THE 5 INGREDIENTS
DIABETiC
COOKBOOK FOR
BEGINNERS

125 Delicious Low Carb Recipes to Reverse
Prediabetes, Balance Blood Sugar For A
Happy & Healthy Life. Incl. Meal Plans
for Prediabetes & Type 2 Diabetes

©PYRIGHT

TABLE OF CONTENTS

CHAPTER 5
SEAFOOD

CHAPTER 6
MEAT AND POULTRY

CHAPTER 7
DESSERTS

MEAL PLANS

INTRODUCTION

Food is one of life's great pleasures. It's alarming to feel that it has become your enemy. Many people become worried about eating after being diagnosed with diabetes. It's normal to lose your confidence in cooking and identifying healthy ingredients. It's not surprising. Most of us grew up hearing the message that fatty food led to becoming overweight. We believed marketing messages around "healthy low-fat products". No one told us that it was refined carbohydrates — and particularly sugar — that was the real enemy.

As someone newly diagnosed with type-2 diabetes, it can be very confusing to find out that the choices you thought were healthy choices were in fact bad for you. And with so much conflicting advice about healthy eating around, it can be difficult to know what your daily meals should look like.

This cookbook is for you. I understand how important it is for diabetics to feel that their needs are met. By focusing on healthy eating in many

ways — far more than just eliminating sugar — I developed a whole set of delicious recipes in which the needs of diabetics are centralized and not just an afterthought to "normal" diets.

This book will restart your health education with scientifically sound dietary guidelines that are especially important for diabetics and pre diabetics to know. By focusing on the best, most up-to-date advice which should help with:

- Preventing prediabetes from becoming full blown type-2 diabetes.
- Keeping type-2 diabetes under manageable control.
- Stabilizing blood glucose levels to less dangerous levels.
- Sending some type-2 diabetic patients into remission, in a best-case scenario.

Best of all, it doesn't mean eating boring food. It's not only possible to eat delicious, healthy food with diabetes, it's not even challenging. I will walk through a few basic scientific guidelines, go through some details of diabetic-friendly ingredients, let you in on some little known hacks, and launch you on your way to making mealtimes a pleasure again — with no worry, no guilt, and no blood sugar spikes.

With only 5 ingredients per recipe — plus a handful of pantry ingredients — and simple, delicious dishes, I will give you back your confidence in grocery shopping, cooking, eating, and enjoying both food and life once more

UNDERSTANDING DIABETES AND DIET

For many people, being diagnosed with type-2 diabetes is an unexpected and frightening set back in their lives. Most of us have spent our lives working hard, trying to live healthily, as much as we can within our busy lives.

In this chapter, I'll walk through why you've been diagnosed, what this diagnosis means and the adjustments you might want to make to your lifestyle and diet. Then you can make sure you go on doing the best you can with the knowledge you have now.

Many people have been on this journey before. Many of them have found themselves able to manage or even in some cases reverse their diabetes through dietary changes.

UNDERSTANDING TYPE-2 DIABETES

What Is Diabetes?

Metabolism is a set of chemical processes that enables our bodies to grow, repair, maintain structure, and adapt to environments. These processes are responsible for converting food to the energy we need to sustain life and bodily functions.

Type-2 diabetes is also known as "insulin insensitivity" or "insulin resistance." It is an acquired medical condition affecting the metabolism.

Our bodies normally use glucose for fuel. After eating, when the body is digesting food, our metabolisms are in an absorptive state, which lasts for a few hours. Nutrients are used for immediate energy, and our bodies convert carbohydrates to glucose. High blood sugar levels trigger insulin release, which promotes uptake of sugar by cells, fat synthesis, and storage of sugar in the liver as glycogen.

Diabetics have a problem either with producing insulin, responding to it correctly, or both. Type-1 diabetics have an auto-immune condition where the insulin-producing cells in the pancreas do not produce insulin. This means they cannot regulate their blood sugar levels in the usual way.

However the tissues of type-2 diabetics typically fail to respond to insulin's message, meaning that blood sugar levels remain high (hyperglycemia). This is the condition known as *insulin insensitivity*. Cells do not take up blood glucose, and consequently the pancreas continues producing insulin. This can then have the extra consequence that the insulin-producing cells in the pancreas become exhausted, and cease to function properly.

In all types of diabetes, it is possible for blood glucose levels to become dangerously variable, which has both short and long-term health risks.

THE ROLE OF DIET

Before insulin was discovered and synthesized, the only option for type-1 diabetics was to manage their diabetes through a low-carbohydrate diet. This was still quite effective: by ensuring that they never ate too many carbohydrates at once, and especially not refined carbohydrates which are quickly converted to blood glucose, diabetics were largely able to prevent their blood sugar levels reaching dangerously high levels. And by carefully timing their next meals, they were also able to effectively manage that it also never got too low.

Compared to the insulin pump technology that type-1 diabetics have access to today, dietary management was a hit-and-miss affair. But it was proven that it was possible to have some degree of control over blood sugar levels through diet alone. This is valuable information for type-2 diabetics today, who suffer primarily from insulin insensitivity, and also for people in the pre-diabetic range who want to get their blood sugar back under control, before they go on to develop full-blown diabetes.

Although there is medication available to help control blood sugar levels, by carefully managing our diet — and especially our intake of carbohydrates — we can manage blood sugar levels more naturally. Many people much prefer to do this, rather than be dependent on medication, which is not only inconvenient but can be expensive.

With careful control of diet, type-2 diabetes should be at worst a manageable health condition. And in the best case scenario, we may even be able to resensitise our bodies to insulin and go into remission from diabetes. By controlling blood sugar, we reduce the need for insulin, giving our insulin-responding tissues a chance to resensitize, and insulin-producing cells in the pancreas a chance for recovery.

How to Control Blood Sugar through Diet

By carefully controlling what types of food we eat and how much of it, we maintain some degree of control over blood glucose levels.

Different types of food raise blood sugar levels at different rates. Carbohydrates are the food that cause blood sugar to rise most quickly. Refined carbohydrates — which are typically stripped of fiber — spike blood glucose most of all, because they are absorbed into the blood so quickly.

By limiting intake of refined carbohydrates and replacing them with whole grain products; focusing on an all-over lower-carb diet and getting more calories in our diet from healthy proteins and fats, we are able to prevent (or at least limit) hyperglycemia, and its associated health risks.

This type of balanced diet, promoting controlled amounts of unrefined carbohydrates, unsaturated fats, and lean protein also has a lot of other health benefits besides controlling blood sugar. It's been linked to better brain health, better cardiovascular health, reduced inflammation, and improved longevity. It's also the diet most consistently linked with healthy weight loss, especially when combined with a lower-calorie diet. Because being overweight is a major risk factor for type-2 diabetes, this diet can have a two-pronged positive effect by assisting in weight loss as well as in control of blood sugar levels.

Remission from Type-2 Diabetes

You may have heard people talking about how it is possible to cure type-2 diabetes, through weight-loss, exercise, healthy diet, and an overall healthy lifestyle.

The term "cure" is misleading; however it is certainly possible to reverse the clinical signs of diabetes and go into a state of remission. With careful control of blood sugar levels through diet, we are also sometimes able to resensitise our bodies to insulin, which further helps with blood sugar control.

The major diagnostic tool used to assess whether someone is diabetic is the HbA1c blood test. This measures glycated hemoglobin (red blood cells that have joined with glucose.) While a blood glucose test measures the blood sugar at any one time, it can be highly variable throughout the day — even minute by minute — and is not a good measure of prolonged hyperglycemia. The HbA1c test is able to give clinicians an overall picture of what average blood glucose levels have been over a period of weeks and months. When HbA1c consistently falls below certain levels, diabetics may be told that their diabetes is in remission.

HbA1c is measured differently in different countries, but in the USA, you'll normally see it given as a percentage. For people without diabetes, the normal HbA1c range is between 4% - 5.6%. Between 5.7% - 6.4 % is the prediabetes range, and levels of 6.5% or higher is the diagnostic standard for diabetes.

If you manage to maintain an HbA1c level of under 6.5% for a sustained period without medication, this is the usual threshold for confirming that your diabetes is in remission.

It's important to monitor your HbA1c levels regularly, but even if these show you have gone into remission, a lower level is not an indication that it is now "safe" for you to revert to a previous high-carb, high-sugar diet. Your lifestyle and dietary changes must be maintained in order to remain in remission.

It's also important to note that with every percentage point increase of HbA1c, the risk of health complications associated with type-2 diabetes increase. Even if your levels remain in the diabetic zone, lower counts within this zone are a lot better than higher ones. It is possible for any diabetic person to experience serious diabetic complications, but the chances of doing so increase dramatically for people with higher levels of HbA1c. Even reducing HbA1c by as little as 1% can still have significant positive health benefits.

General Health and Well-Being

The recommended eating pattern for type-2 diabetics comes with a large number of other health benefits. Carbohydrates are a valuable source of energy and should not be completely eliminat-

ed, but it is important for them to be consumed in moderation, and together with fiber, fat, and protein. Ensuring your diet is correctly balanced between these nutrients is the key to good health.

For many years, we were recommended to get approximately half of our daily calories from starchy carbohydrates, and to consume only small amounts of fat. However, more recent studies show that a much more moderate consumption of carbohydrates is better for health in multiple ways, and especially when it comes to blood sugar control.

Far from being a demon, fat is a crucial component of our diets, being required for the absorption of fat-soluble vitamins, aiding brain development, providing structure to cell membranes, and maintaining healthy hair and skin. Saturated fats from animal products are associated with risks to cardiovascular health; therefore, it's better to choose unsaturated "heart-healthy" fats, like olive oil. Fat is also calorie-dense, so should be consumed in moderation; however a diet that is ultra-low in fat is generally not recommended.

Vegetables (and, to a lesser degree, fruit) should form the majority part of our diet. It's also advisable to limit starchy vegetables, like potatoes, which can also lead to blood sugar spikes. As well as vitamins and minerals, non-starchy vegetables also contain large amounts of dietary fiber, aiding digestion, and inhibiting blood sugar spikes. They also contain antioxidants with powerful anti-inflammatory properties.

Protein is essential for building and repairing muscles and bones, and manufacturing hormones; however it can come along with unwelcome saturated fat (especially meat.) Lean animal proteins, or vegetable proteins are advised to form the bulk of our protein intake.

By following these general guidelines, you are likely to find that your overall health improves. You are likely to see measurable reductions in blood pressure, blood sugar, blood cholesterol, and inflammatory markers. Brain health and mental acuity are improved, and many people also report feeling more energetic, with better skin and hair, better digestion, and better sleep.

You are, of course, also far less likely to experience diabetes-related complications, and you have a good chance of being able to reverse your clinical symptoms and go into remission.

COMMON MYTHS

There are a lot of myths and bad advice circulating about diets suitable for diabetics. I covered all this in detail in this book, but for quick reference, here are five common myths you may have read or heard, and be concerned about:

1. **Myth: No more carbs. Ever.**

Fact: Carbohydrates are often misunderstood. While they can raise blood sugar levels, they can still be included in a diabetic diet in moderation. It's important to choose high-fiber, healthy carb sources like whole grains, fruits, and vegetables, and to manage portion sizes.

2. **Myth: Fruit is off-limits.**

Fact: Fruits contain natural sugars but are also rich in essential nutrients and fiber. People with diabetes can enjoy fruits, especially those lower in sugar like berries and apples, as part of a balanced diet.

3. **Myth: All fats are bad.**

Fact: Not all fats are detrimental to health. Healthy fats, such as those found in avocados, nuts, and fish, are important for bodily functions. It's crucial to limit unhealthy fats, like saturated and trans fats, but including healthy fats in moderation is beneficial.

4. **Myth: If I'm on medication, I can eat whatever I want.**

Fact: Medication helps manage blood sugar levels, but it does not replace the need for a balanced diet. Consuming unhealthy foods can counteract the benefits of medication and hinder diabetes management.

5. **Myth: I need to lose a lot of weight immediately.**

Fact: Significant weight loss is not necessary to see improvements in diabetes management. Even a modest weight loss of 5-10% of body weight can have a positive impact on blood sugar control and overall health

PRACTICAL DIETARY GUIDANCE FOR DIABETICS

So what does all this mean from a practical point of view? It's all very well to learn about the importance of avoiding glucose spikes, but what should that look like in your grocery basket and on your plate? Let's dive into the details.

What to Eat

Most of your diet should consist of non-starchy vegetables, legumes, and lean protein. Legumes do contain carbs, but also a lot of fiber and protein, making them a healthy choice for diabetics. You can also use legume-derived products, such as tofu.

Herbs and spices, although not usually consumed in bulk, may also be used to add flavor.

Low-starch vegetables, e.g.

- Garlic
- Zucchini
- Broccoli
- Cauliflower
- Leafy greens
- Asparagus
- Cucumber
- Celery
- Cabbage
- Tomatoes
- Avocados
- Eggplant
- Bell peppers
- Fennel

Legumes and derivatives, e.g.

- Beans
- Lentils
- Chickpeas
- Split peas
- Tofu

Lean protein

- White meat chicken
- Lean beef
- Lean pork
- Fish
- Shrimp
- Shellfish
- Eggs

Herbs and Spices, e.g.

- Cumin
- Turmeric
- Coriander
- Paprika
- Cinnamon
- Nutmeg
- Ginger
- Parsley
- Cilantro

- Sage
- Rosemary
- Thyme
- Dill
- Basil

What to Eat In Moderation

You can eat complex, unrefined carbohydrates, but even these should be carefully counted and controlled. The important thing to count is the **NET CARBS**; this means the total carbohydrates less the fiber. Fiber is a carbohydrate, but it does not contribute to blood glucose levels in any way.

You also need to have healthy unsaturated fats in your diet. But because all fats are calorie-dense (yielding an average of 9 calories per gram of fat, compared to 4 calories per gram for protein and carbs), you need to be careful about how much you consume, especially if on a calorie-controlled diet. Nuts and seeds are an important source of micronutrients, but their high fat content means they also need to be consumed in moderation.

Unsweetened dairy products may also be eaten, being rich in protein and minerals. Fermented products are particularly good. However, they do contain saturated fats as well, so should be consumed only moderately (or low-fat versions.) The same is true for meat with a higher fat proportion: brown meat chicken; most cuts of pork; and many cuts of red meat. They have value, but caution is advised due to the saturated fat content.

Lastly, higher-fiber fruits contain a lot of vitamins and antioxidants making them an important part of a healthy diet. But the sugar content is still high enough that portion control is advised. A general rule of thumb for fruit is to consume portions containing an absolute maximum of 15 g of carbohydrates. In practical terms, this translates to half a medium apple, 1 medium fig, 1 cup of raspberries, 1 small nectarine, or a small orange. It's sensible to combine them with other ingredients that are rich in protein or fiber, to limit blood sugar spikes.

Whole grain carbs and starchy vegetables, e.g.

- Whole wheat pasta
- Whole grain flour
- Brown rice
- Potatoes

- Sweet potatoes
- Squash
- Corn

Dairy and meat, e.g.

- Milk
- Unsweetened yogurt
- Buttermilk
- Kefir
- Cheese
- Most cuts of pork
- Brown meat chicken and skin
- Many cuts of red meat

Nuts and seeds, e.g.

- Almonds
- Peanuts
- Pumpkin seeds

Higher-fiber fruits, e.g.

- Berries
- Cherries
- Figs
- Oranges
- Apples
- Pears
- Nectarines

Lower-sugar fruits, e.g.

- Berries

Unsaturated fats, e.g.

- Olive oil

What to Avoid

Any foods that are high in sugar or other refined carbohydrates are likely to raise blood glucose levels quickly, leading to a spike, and are therefore best avoided or consumed in strict moderation. This includes high-sugar fruits.

Extreme caution is also advised around the con-sumption of highly processed or packaged items, which often contain added sugars, fats, or other additives that can be harmful to health.

Any items which are high in saturated fats, or contain trans fats are also best avoided.

High sugar items, e.g.

- Sugar
- Honey
- Molasses
- Maple syrup
- Dates
- Dried fruit

Refined carbohydrates and derivatives, e.g.

- White rice
- White flour
- White bread
- White pasta

High-sugar fruits, e.g.

- Bananas
- Watermelon
- Grapes
- Pineapples
- Mangos
- Watermelon

Some fats, e.g.

- Saturated fats
- Trans fats

Processed goods, e.g.

- Pastries
- Cakes
- Candy
- Breakfast cereals
- Cookies
- Potato chips
- Corn chips
- Processed meats

High-fat dairy, e.g.

- Butter
- Cream
- Sour cream

Portion Control

With all ingredients, no matter what category they fall in, the key is moderation. When we say some items are best avoided, we don't mean that you must never eat them. You will even find a few recipes in this book that contain some of these ingredients. What is advised is that they are eaten in very small quantities, and together with other ingredients that mitigate their immediate effect on blood glucose levels.

Likewise, just because some ingredients are on the "safe" list does not mean you can eat them in abundance with no regard for portion control. Overeating of any item is not advised.

The exact amount you will want to consume depends on your particular situation: your body weight; your exercise levels; and your weight-loss goals. Diabetic or not, most of us eat larger portions than is advisable, so it is likely that sensible portions will appear small to you at first.

If you're not sure about how much to eat, or in what proportions, a good rule of thumb is that half of your plate should consist of non-starchy vegetables, a quarter of lean protein, and the remaining quarter should be legumes, starchy vegetables, or whole grain carbohydrates.

The average advised protein portion per meal is approximately 3 ounces, equivalent to the size of a deck of playing cards, or the palm of your hand.

If you are diabetic but not following a lower-calorie diet, it is usually advisable to reduce the proportion of carbohydrates further, and get more of your calories from vegetables and lean protein.

Useful Hacks

As well as the generalized eating guidelines advised for diabetics — portion control, counting (and limiting) carbohydrates — there are also a number of things you can do that have surprisingly large and beneficial effects on your blood sugar levels.

High-Protein Breakfast

It's especially important to be careful about what you consume for breakfast. Our bodies naturally have higher blood sugar levels in the mornings to help us wake up — this is known as the *dawn phenomenon* — and diabetics are unable to control it through insulin release in the normal way. So it's vital not to exacerbate these already-elevated blood glucose levels by consuming a high-carb breakfast.

Focus on a high protein breakfast, which will fill you up, and keep you feeling fuller for longer. As those morning blood sugar levels decline, the protein steps up with slow-release energy, keeping blood glucose relatively stable, and maintaining mental acuity without the need for caffeinated or sugary drinks throughout the day.

Vinegar

This is a relatively new finding, but there is some tentative evidence to suggest that consuming vinegar with carbohydrates (or shortly beforehand) reduces the absorption rate, and is associated with a slower increase and more stable blood glucose levels. The exact mechanism is not fully understood, but it is thought that vinegar delays gastric emptying. It has been found to be particularly effective when consumed with more complex carbohydrates. Try adding a tablespoon of apple cider vinegar to a glass of water and drinking it directly before your meal.

Start with Vegetables

Before your main dish, eat an appetizer of vegetables. The order in which you eat food has been shown to have a surprisingly large effect both on how quickly glucose is absorbed into the blood, and also on ghrelin — the hormone that controls appetite and lets you know when you are hungry. Find out more information about this in the bonus eBook, which also includes 50 great recipes for veggie appetizers!

Eating Food in the Right Order

It's not only starting with vegetables, the order in which you eat the rest of your food also affects blood glucose levels during the postprandial absorption period. The high fiber foods — usually vegetables — should come first, followed by the proteins and fats, and finally the carbs. Some studies have shown that eating meals in the correct order led to reductions of up to 73% in blood sugar spikes, compared to participants who ate the exact same meal in a different order.

Exercise after Eating Carbs

Being active after eating carbs is a way to reduce blood sugar naturally by diverting all that energy directly into muscle movement. The more energetic we are, the greater the energy usage, and the more sugar is used. It doesn't even have to be a full workout. Just walking for as little as ten minutes has been shown to have a significant effect on reducing blood glucose levels after eating.

Mimicking Sweetness

This hack is less about reducing blood sugar levels than about reducing cravings for sugar. It can be really hard to reduce sugar in your diet. Our bodies are hardwired to crave it, as a quick and easy source of energy. This would once have been of evolutionary benefit, when food sources could be scarce.

But you can trick your tastebuds into thinking food is sweeter than it is, which helps to alleviate sugar cravings. Artificial sweeteners are one way to do this, although they should only be used in moderation, as some studies have found links between excessive consumption of artificial sweeteners and obesity.

The other, more natural hack is to add ingredients that we associate with sweetness. Vanilla, cinnamon, and nutmeg are all ingredients that can trick us into perceiving sweetness, even at very low levels of sugar content.

Adding Flavor

Although there is no reason why a diet suitable for diabetics should be lacking in flavor, you may find it difficult to make a switch from the diet you have been accustomed to. Processed foods in particular are packed full of flavor enhancers as well as salt, unhealthy fat, and sugar. It can take a week or so for your taste buds to "reset" and stop finding these additives necessary for flavor. This is especially true for salt.

If you're finding food is initially tasting a bit bland, your main hack here is herbs and spices. They provide pops of intense flavor and successfully distract you from the lack of salt. Another trick is to add a little acidity. You will be amazed at how much a squeeze of fresh lemon juice brightens the flavor of a dish.

MEAL PLANNING

You may have heard or read about "decision fatigue". This refers to the mental energy required to make decisions — even very basic ones — about what to wear, which store to visit, and what to eat. When we're tired, we find it hard to make decisions, and even harder to choose something that is different to normal. It's far easier, mentally, to default to the normal.

You can immediately imagine how this can scupper your best intentions when commencing a new healthy diet. So don't make your decisions about what to eat on a day-by-day basis. That way you are far more likely to be too tired to decide on the new healthy option, and default to your normal, high-carb, unhealthy option.

Instead, make the time to sit down for half an hour, once a week, and plan out all of your meals for the week at once. That way, you won't have to make the decision when tired, you only need to consult the plan.

Weekly Planning

When you do your weekly plan, don't be too ambitious. By that, I mean don't set yourself unrealistic targets. An ultra-low calorie diet is very hard; better to ease into a lower-calorie diet to start with and keep it up.

And almost no one cooks a full meal for themselves three times a day, plus homemade snacks! Home cooked food is good — you know exactly what goes into it. But no one wants to spend hours in the kitchen every day. Be realistic about what you can achieve. There are some tips below about batch cooking that you may find useful.

Lastly, plan for your weak moments as well. There will be a time when you're hungry and tired and you just want SOMETHING. You are going to reach for something that satisfies your cravings, so make sure you've got a *healthy* snack at hand that will do the job. Just a small pack of unsalted nuts, or some crunchy vegetable crudités will be enough.

Grocery Shopping

When you're doing your weekly meal plan, write your grocery list at the same time. Then when you get to the store, you know exactly what to buy and won't be distracted into unhealthy impulse purchases. If it's not on the list, you don't buy it!

Remember to write down the quantities you want for the week as well. For non-perishable items, it's often cheaper to buy in bulk — but you want to be aware for your portion control that you'll only be using (e.g.) one quarter of that bag of rice in the week to come.

As discussed above, the large majority of your food should consist of fresh vegetables, pulses, and lean protein — all items with zero or minimal processing. To a lesser degree, dairy, nuts, and other healthy fat sources. There should be very few packaged, processed items in your grocery cart.

When choosing between different options, don't assume that bold statements on the front of the packaging like "low-fat" or "healthy" or "no added sugar" mean the product is suitable for you. Instead, check the ingredients list and nutritional table to find out the exact sugar content and ingredients. Beware of "secret sugars" that hide under a different name. Cane sugar, honey, brown sugar, high-fructose corn syrup, fruit juice concentrate, fruit purée, corn syrup, fructose, sucrose, glucose, crystalline sucrose, nectars, maple syrup, agave syrup, dextrose, maltose, molasses and treacle are all examples. This is another reason to avoid packaged foods, which are more likely to have unfamiliar ingredients in them. If in doubt, leave it out!

Batch Cooking

Some people find this an absolute game-changer in terms of healthy eating. As well as planning out your meals for the week, plan to cook double (or more) and refrigerate or freeze some portions for future use. That way, you'll always have a healthy meal at hand, for days when you just don't have the energy to cook.

Some cooks like to take it further still and allocate a couple of hours once a week to prepare a whole week (or even more) of meals in advance. This limits the amount of time required to spend in the kitchen day-to-day, and frees up time for other things. You do need to be more organized, but once you've got the hang of it, it can be literally transformative to your cooking and diet.

ABOUT THIS COOKBOOK

I know it can be hard to get started with something new. That's why I'm making it easy for you with this cookbook. When you're trying to figure out a whole new way of healthy eating, the last thing you need is to have to get to grips with complicated new ingredients or cooking techniques as well!

In all recipes, simplicity and flavor were paramount. I want these recipes not only to be delicious and healthy but also to be quick and simple. Most of them take under 30 minutes to prepare — many of them less than 15 minutes. The few that do take longer are mostly cooking time, not active prep time, meaning they are "set and forget" dishes. They will happily cook to perfection in the oven or on the stove while you can relax, or get on with other chores.

The 5 Ingredient Approach

As well as simplicity of preparation, I also wanted to keep grocery shopping to a minimum. That's why you'll find that all dishes can be prepared with only five fresh ingredients to add to your grocery list. Additionally, I assumed you'll have a small number of pantry ingredients that can be added to enhance those five fresh ingredients, and make that simplicity simply super!

Staple Pantry Items

All recipes in this book can be made with just five fresh ingredients, plus additional small quantities from the following staple pantry items:

Spices

- Salt
- Pepper
- Ras el hanout
- Garam masala
- Italian seasoning

Oil and vinegar

- Olive oil
- Neutral flavor vegetable oil
- Extra virgin olive oil
- Apple cider vinegar

Other

- Reduced sodium soy sauce
- Tomato paste
- Chili paste (e.g. harissa)
- Baking powder
- Vanilla extract

YOUR FREE GIFT

Scan the QR code to download the complimentary eBooks. We promise you will love them!

CHAPTER 1
BREAKFAST

ALMOND PANCAKES WITH STRAWBERRIES

vegetarian, gluten-free, lactose-free

 SERVES: 2

 PREP TIME: 5 MINUTES

 COOK TIME: 5 MINUTES

5 INGREDIENTS

- ⅔ cup (80 g) almond flour
- 1 medium egg, plus 1 yolk
- ¼ tsp vanilla extract
- 1 cup (150 g) of strawberries, hulled and sliced
- 1 tbsp sliced almonds, toasted

From the pantry
- ½ tsp baking powder
- 1 pinch of salt
- 2 tbsp olive oil for frying

METHOD

1. Whisk the almond flour, egg, yolk, vanilla, baking powder and salt together, along with ¼ cup of water, to form a batter.
2. Put the oil into a large non-stick skillet and set over medium-high heat.
3. Ladle approx 1 tbsp of batter per pancake into the hot skillet, and allow to spread out to about 2 inch diameter.
4. Flip once you see bubbles forming on the top, and cook for just 30 seconds-1 minute on the reverse side. Repeat until you have used all the batter; should make about 8 in total.
5. Put 4 pancakes on each plate, and garnish with the strawberries and sliced almonds. Enjoy!
6. TIP: Swap out the strawberries for any other berries you might like!

Nutritional Values, estimated per serving: Macros: Protein 11% / Fat 75% / Carbs 14%; Calories: 425 | Total carbs: 15 g | Net carbs: 9 g | Sugar: 6 g | Protein 13 g | Fat: 37 g | Saturated fat: 5 g | Cholesterol: 174 mg | Sodium: 38 mg; Glycemic Load: 2.0

AVOCADO TOAST WITH ASPARAGUS AND EGGS

vegetarian, lactose-free

 SERVES: 2

 PREP TIME: 5 MINUTES

 COOK TIME: 8 MINUTES

5 INGREDIENTS

- 4 thin slices whole grain bread
- 1 medium avocado, peeled and stone removed
- 4 medium eggs
- 12 spears of asparagus, woody ends cut off
- 1 cup (160 g) peas

From the pantry
- 1 tbsp olive oil
- Salt
- Pepper

METHOD

1. Bring a large pan of salted water to a boil, then add the asparagus. Cook for about 5 minutes, until slightly softened, but still retaining some "bite". Add the peas to the water when there are just 2 minutes remaining.
2. Meanwhile, toast the bread, mash and season the avocado, and spread it onto the toast.
3. Heat 1 tbsp olive oil in a non-stick skillet and fry the eggs until done to your liking.
4. Lay 3 asparagus spears on each piece of toast, scatter over the peas, and top with the fried eggs. Enjoy!
5. TIP: If you like it zingy, try squeezing over a little lemon juice!

Nutritional Values, estimated per serving: Macros: Protein 18% / Fat 56% / Carbs 26%; Calories: 429 | Total carbs: 28 g | Net carbs: 19 g | Sugar: 6 g | Protein 19 g | Fat: 31 g | Saturated fat: 4 g | Cholesterol: 327 mg | Sodium: 525 mg; Glycemic Load: 11.37

SMASHED AVOCADO WITH EDAMAME

vegan, gluten-free, lactose-free

 SERVES: 2

 PREP TIME: 5 MINUTES

COOK TIME: 0 MINUTES

5 INGREDIENTS

- 1 avocado, peeled and stone removed
- 1 cup (160 g) cooked edamame beans
- ¼ cup (40 g) roasted red peppers, sliced
- ½ lemon, zest and juice
- 2 small slices whole grain bread, toasted

From the pantry
- 1 tsp olive oil
- Salt

METHOD

1. Crush the avocado roughly with the edamame beans, olive oil, lemon juice and zest, and a small pinch of salt. Mix in the red peppers.
2. Toast or grill the bread, and serve alongside the smashed avocado sauce.
3. TIP: Mix in some additional leafy greens for extra fiber! Spinach, arugula, or lettuce would all be great.

Nutritional Values, estimated per serving: Macros: Protein 16% / Fat 50% / Carbs 34%; Calories: 304 | Total carbs: 27 g | Net carbs: 16 g | Sugar: 5 g | Protein 13 g | Fat: 18 g | Saturated fat: 2 g | Cholesterol: 0 mg | Sodium: 400 mg; Glycemic Load: 10.92

OVERNIGHT OATS WITH ALMONDS AND RASPBERRIES

vegetarian, gluten-free

 SERVES: 4

 PREP TIME: 5 MINUTES

 COOK TIME: 0 MINUTES

5 INGREDIENTS

- ½ cup (50 g) rolled oats
- 1 cup (240 ml) almond milk (or even water, if you trying to go as low-cal as possible)
- 1 cup (230 g) Greek yogurt
- ½ cup (40 g) roughly chopped almonds
- 1 cup (125 g) raspberries

METHOD

1. Mix the oats with the almond milk, the almonds, and the Greek yogurt. Split between 4 Mason jars or glasses, and refrigerate overnight.
2. The following morning, top with the raspberries.
3. TIP: Try swapping the raspberries for a fresh apple, if you like! It raises the net carbs a bit, but only by about an extra 4 g.

Nutritional Values, estimated per serving: Macros: Protein 22% / Fat 35% / Carbs 43%; Calories: 188 | Total carbs: 20 g | Net carbs: 15 g | Sugar: 8 g | Protein 8 g | Fat: 9 g | Saturated fat: 2 g | Cholesterol:8 mg | Sodium: 57 mg; Glycemic Load: 5.62

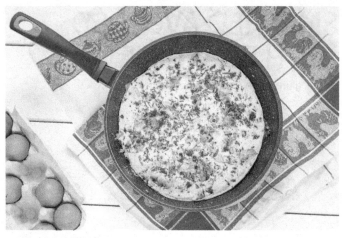

SPINACH AND FETA OMELETTE

vegetarian, gluten-free

 SERVES: 2

 PREP TIME: 5 MINUTES

 COOK TIME: 5 MINUTES

5 INGREDIENTS

- 2 medium eggs, and 4 egg whites
- 1 cup (30 g) spinach, shredded
- 2 oz (60 g) feta, crumbled
- 1 sprig of dill, finely chopped
- ½ cup (120 g) cooked pumpkin, diced

From the pantry
- 1 tbsp olive oil
- Salt and pepper
- 1 tsp Italian seasoning

METHOD

1. Beat the eggs and egg whites together with the spinach and the Italian seasoning, and add a pinch of salt and pepper.
2. Heat the olive oil in a non-stick skillet over medium heat, then pour in the eggs.
3. Scatter over the pumpkin and feta, then put a lid on the skillet.
4. Cook for about 3-4 minutes, until set on top, and lightly browned underneath.
5. Scatter with the dill, and serve. Enjoy!
6. TIP: If you like your breakfast spicy, add a finely diced red chili pepper, or a pinch of red pepper flakes!

Nutritional Values, estimated per serving: Macros: Protein 30 % / Fat 61 % / Carbs 9 %; Calories: 252 | Total carbs: 6 g | Net carbs: 5 g | Sugar: 3 g | Protein 18 g | Fat: 17 g | Saturated fat: 7 g | Cholesterol: 189 mg | Sodium: 840 mg; Glycemic Load: 3.39

GRIBICHE ON ToAST

vegetarian, lactose-free

 SERVES: 2

 PREP TIME: 5 MINUTES

 COOK TIME: 10 MINUTES

5 INGREDIENTS

- 4 medium eggs
- 2 large dill pickles, finely diced
- 1 sprig tarragon, finely chopped
- 2 tbsp capers, finely chopped
- 2 thin slices of whole grain bread

From the pantry
- 1 tbsp olive oil
- Pepper

METHOD

1. Bring a pan of water to a boil, and boil the eggs for 8-10 minutes, until the whites are set and the yolks are jammy. Peel, and separate the yolks from the whites.
2. Mix the egg yolks with the olive oil until smooth and emulsified.
3. Roughly chop the egg whites, and mix with the dill pickles, capers, and tarragon. Fold in the egg yolk mixture. Season with pepper only; the capers and pickles are salty enough.
4. Toast the bread, and serve together with the egg gribiche. Enjoy!
5. TIP: Any soft herbs are good in gribiche. Try mixing it up with parsley, basil, chives, chervil, etc.

Nutritional Values, estimated per serving: Macros: Protein 23% / Fat 54% / Carbs 22%; Calories: 275 | Total carbs: 16 g | Net carbs: 12 g | Sugar: 3 g | Protein 16 g | Fat: 17 g | Saturated fat: 4 g | Cholesterol: 327 mg | Sodium: 1519 mg; Glycemic Load: 6.13

AVOCADO TOAST WITH RYE BREAD

vegetarian

 SERVES: 2

 PREP TIME: 5 MINUTES

 COOK TIME: 0 MINUTES

5 INGREDIENTS

- 1 medium avocado, peeled, stone removed, and sliced
- 1 tbsp sesame seeds, toasted
- 1 tbsp pumpkin seeds, toasted
- 2 tbsp cream cheese, fat free, if you like
- 2 slices of whole grain rye bread

From the pantry
- Salt and pepper

METHOD

1. Spread the cream cheese on the rye bread, and season with salt and pepper.
2. Put the sliced avocado on top, and scatter with the seeds. Enjoy!
3. TIP: If you're avoiding gluten, try swapping the rye bread for whole grain gluten-free bread!

Nutritional Values, estimated per serving: Macros: Protein 13% / Fat 58% / Carbs 29%; Calories: 295 | Total carbs: 22 g | Net carbs: 13 g | Sugar: 2 g | Protein 10 g | Fat: 20 g | Saturated fat: 3 g | Cholesterol: 2 mg | Sodium: 526 mg; Glycemic Load: 7.22

SUMMER FRITTATA

vegetarian, gluten-free

 SERVES: 2

 PREP TIME: 10 MINUTES

 COOK TIME: 5 MINUTES

5 INGREDIENTS

- 4 medium eggs
- 1 medium zucchini, grated
- 1 carrot, grated
- 2 oz (60 g) feta, crumbled
- 1 cup (20 g) arugula

From the pantry
- 1 tbsp olive oil
- Salt and pepper

METHOD

1. Squeeze as much liquid out of the grated vegetables as you can, then mix with the beaten eggs and season lightly.
2. Heat the olive oil in a non-stick skillet over medium heat, then pour in the egg mix.
3. Cook for about 3-4 minutes, until lightly browned underneath, then carefully flip, and cook for another 2 minutes on the reverse side.
4. Turn out of the pan, scatter with the feta and rucola, and enjoy!
5. TIP: If you're into juicing, save the liquid from the squeezed vegetables, and add to your next morning juice for some extra nourishment!

Nutritional Values, estimated per serving: Macros: Protein 24% / Fat 66% / Carbs 10%; Calories: 292 | Total carbs: 8 g | Net carbs: 6 g | Sugar: 6 g | Protein 17 g | Fat: 21 g | Saturated fat: 8 g | Cholesterol: 353 mg | Sodium: 533 mg; Glycemic Load: 4.21

CAULIFLOWER HASH BROWNS

vegetarian, lactose-free

 SERVES: 2

 PREP TIME: 10 MINUTES

 COOK TIME: 5 MINUTES

5 INGREDIENTS

- 1 small cauliflower, florets only, grated
- 2 medium eggs
- 1 medium onion, peeled and finely sliced
- ½ cup (125 g) mashed potato
- 1 tbsp garlic powder

From the pantry

- 1 tbsp olive oil
- 1 tbsp whole wheat flour
- salt and pepper

METHOD

1. Mix the cauliflower, eggs, onion, potato, garlic powder, and flour together. Season with salt and pepper.
2. Heat the olive oil in a non-stick skillet over medium heat, and add dollops of the mix, pressing lightly to flatten into rough patties.
3. Fry for about 3 minutes, until golden brown on the underside, then flip, and cook for a further 2 minutes on the reverse side. Be careful when flipping, they are quite delicate.
4. Turn out of the pan, and enjoy while hot!
5. TIP: These also make a good lower carb side dish for a lunch or dinner!

Nutritional Values, estimated per serving: Macros: Protein 16% / Fat 43% / Carbs 41%; Calories: 236 | Total carbs: 25 g | Net carbs: 20 g | Sugar: 6 g | Protein 10 g | Fat: 11 g | Saturated fat: 3 g | Cholesterol: 164 mg | Sodium: 690 mg; Glycemic Load: 12.83

COCOA PEANUT CHIA PUDDING

vegetarian, gluten-free

 SERVES: 4

 PREP TIME: 10 MINUTES

 CHILL TIME: OVERNIGHT

5 INGREDIENTS

- 6 tbsp chia seeds
- 1 cup (240 ml) full-fat milk (or unsweetened nut milk if you prefer plant-based)
- 1 cup (230 g) Greek yogurt
- 2 tbsp smooth peanut butter
- 3 tbsp unsweetened cocoa powder, plus a little extra to dust.

From the pantry

- A pinch of salt
- ½ tsp vanilla extract

METHOD

1. Mix the chia seeds with the milk, yogurt, peanut butter, cocoa powder, vanilla extract, and a pinch of salt. Chill for a few hours, then stir well to break up any lumps, and split between 4 mason jars. Continue chilling overnight.
2. Dust the pudding with a little extra cocoa powder just before serving.
3. TIP: Make the pudding while you prepare dinner, and stir just before you go to bed. Top with a few healthy blueberries, and some chopped peanuts if you like!

Nutritional Values, estimated per serving: Macros: Protein 23% / Fat 47% / Carbs 30%; Calories: 235 | Total carbs: 19 g | Net carbs: 10 g | Sugar: 6 g | Protein 15 g | Fat: 13 g | Saturated fat: 3 g | Cholesterol: 8 mg | Sodium: 134 mg; Glycemic Load: 3.46

BREAKFAST SALAD WiTH SMOKED SALMON

pescetarian, gluten-free, lactose-free

 SERVES: 2

PREP TIME: 5 MINUTES

 COOK TIME: 10 MINUTES

5 INGREDIENTS

- 2 cups (40 g) arugula
- 2 medium eggs
- 4 oz (110 g) smoked salmon
- 1 medium avocado, peeled, stone removed, and sliced
- 1 medium lemon, juice and zest

From the pantry
- 1 tbsp olive oil
- ½ tsp Italian seasoning
- Salt and pepper

METHOD

1. Bring a pan of water to a boil and boil the eggs for 8-10 minutes, until the whites are set and the yolks are jammy. Peel and halve.
2. Mix the olive oil with the Italian seasoning, the lemon juice and zest and season to taste.
3. Split the arugula, avocado, and salmon between the two serving plates, top with two halves of a boiled egg on each, and pour over the dressing. Enjoy!
4. TIP: Scatter over some sesame seeds for Hawaiian Poke Bowl vibes!

Nutritional Values, estimated per serving: Macros: Protein 21% / Fat 68% / Carbs 11%; Calories: 362 | Total carbs: 12 g | Net carbs: 5 g | Sugar: 2 g | Protein 19 g | Fat: 28 g | Saturated fat: 5 g | Cholesterol: 177 mg | Sodium: 507 mg; Glycemic Load: 2.76

SPANISH ToRTiLLA

vegetarian, gluten-free

 SERVES: 2

 PREP TIME: 5 MINUTES

 COOK TIME: 12 MINUTES

5 INGREDIENTS

- 1 cup (150 g) cooked potatoes, diced
- 1 medium onion, peeled and sliced
- 2 cups (60 g) of raw spinach, chopped
- 1 red bell pepper, sliced
- 4 medium eggs

From the pantry
- 2 tsp olive oil
- Salt and pepper to taste

METHOD

1. Warm half the olive oil in a small pan and sauté the onion and red bell pepper for about 5 minutes, until softened, but not colored.
2. Add the spinach, and stir through just until it wilts, only 1 minute.
3. In a large mixing bowl, add the onions, bell peppers, and spinach to the cooked potatoes. Stir to combine, then add the eggs and season to taste.
4. Warm the other half of the olive oil in the same skillet, over medium-low heat, tip the mixture in and smooth the top.
5. Fry for about 3-4 minutes, until set around the edges. Carefully invert the tortilla pan over an upturned plate, then slide it back into the pan to cook the reverse side.
6. Cook for just a minute or two until set. Serve immediately.
7. TIP: Vary up the veg! You can add any vegetables at all to the potato egg mixture!

Nutritional Values, estimated per serving: Macros: Protein 21% / Fat 42% / Carbs 37%; Calories: 280 | Total carbs: 26 g | Net carbs: 22 g | Sugar: 6 g | Protein 14 g | Fat: 13 g | Saturated fat: 3 g | Cholesterol: 327 mg | Sodium: 157 mg; Glycemic Load: 13.10

BROCCOLI MUFFINS WITH CHEDDAR

vegetarian, gluten-free

 SERVES: 4 (3 MUFFINS EACH)

 PREP TIME: 10 MINUTES

 COOK TIME: 25 MINUTES

5 INGREDIENTS

- 4 medium eggs, and 6 egg whites
- ½ cup (50 g) cheddar cheese, grated
- 1 small head of broccoli, broken into florets
- 4 scallions, sliced
- 1 tsp garlic powder

From the pantry
- Salt and pepper
- Olive oil to grease the muffin tins

METHOD

1. Preheat the oven to 350°F. Grease a 12-hole muffin tin with olive oil.
2. Steam the broccoli for about 4 minutes until cooked, and break it up into smaller pieces.
3. Beat the eggs, cheese, scallions and garlic powder together, and season.
4. Beat the egg whites alone, until frothy and holding soft peaks, then fold into the cheese mixture.
5. Divide the broccoli between the 12 holes of the muffin tin, then pour in the egg mix.
6. Bake for about 20 minutes until golden brown. Enjoy!
7. TIP: Try with a different type of cheese for a change. Stilton is very good with broccoli!

Nutritional Values, estimated per serving: Macros: Protein 31% / Fat 50% / Carbs 19%; Calories: 235 | Total carbs: 13 g | Net carbs: 9 g | Sugar: 4 g | Protein 19 g | Fat: 13 g | Saturated fat: 5 g | Cholesterol: 178 mg | Sodium: 579 mg; Glycemic Load: 2.07

RICOTTA TOAST WITH STRAWBERRIES

vegetarian

 SERVES: 2

 PREP TIME: 5 MINUTES

 COOK TIME: 1 MINUTE

5 INGREDIENTS

- 2 slices whole grain bread
- 3 tbsp ricotta
- 1 cup (150 g) strawberries, hulled and sliced
- 1 sprig of basil, shredded
- 2 tbsp unsalted pistachios, shelled and roughly chopped

From the pantry
- 1 tbsp olive oil
- Freshly ground black pepper

METHOD

1. Toast the bread, then spread with the ricotta.
2. Drizzle with the olive oil, then scatter over the strawberries, basil, and pistachios.
3. Grind over some black pepper and enjoy!
4. TIP: Regular cream cheese is a nice variation, if you can't get hold of ricotta!

Nutritional Values, estimated per serving: Macros: Protein 14% / Fat 53% / Carbs 33%; Calories: 240 | Total carbs: 21 g | Net carbs: 17 g | Sugar: 6 g | Protein 8 g | Fat: 15 g | Saturated fat: 4 g | Cholesterol: 12 mg | Sodium: 120 mg; Glycemic Load: 11.52

MEXICAN SCRAMBLED EGGS

vegetarian, gluten-free

 SERVES: 4

 PREP TIME: 5 MINUTES

 COOK TIME: 10 MINUTES

5 INGREDIENTS

- 1 medium red onion, peeled and chopped
- 1 green bell pepper, sliced
- 2 medium tomatoes, chopped
- 6 medium eggs, beaten
- 1 small bunch cilantro, roughly chopped

From the pantry
- 1 tsp olive oil
- 1 tsp chili paste (optional)
- Salt and pepper to taste

METHOD

1. Warm the olive oil in a small pan over medium heat and sauté the onion and green bell pepper for about 5 minutes, until softened, but not colored.
2. Add the tomatoes, cook for another 3 minutes, then turn the heat down low.
3. Mix the eggs with the chili paste (if using), season to taste, and add to the pan.
4. Cook for about 2 minutes, stirring all the time, until the eggs are scrambled and cooked to your liking.
5. Stir in the cilantro, and serve.
6. TIP: Optionally add tortillas on the side, but be careful – they can be very high in carbs. Look out for low-carb versions.

Nutritional Values, estimated per serving: Macros: Protein 32% / Fat 53% / Carbs 15%; Calories: 183 | Total carbs: 7 g | Net carbs: 5 g | Sugar: 3 g | Protein 14 g | Fat: 11 g | Saturated fat: 3 g | Cholesterol: 372 mg | Sodium: 313 mg; Glycemic Load: 3.46

BAKED AVOCADO WITH EGGS

vegetarian, gluten-free, lactose-free

 SERVES: 2

 PREP TIME: 5 MINUTES

 COOK TIME: 15 MINUTES

5 INGREDIENTS

- 2 medium avocados
- 4 small eggs
- 1 sprig of parsley, roughly chopped
- ¼ tsp red pepper flakes
- 1 lemon

From the pantry
- Salt and pepper

METHOD

1. Preheat the oven to 425°F.
2. Halve the avocados and remove the stones. Put a pinch of red pepper flakes in each cavity, and crack the eggs in. Season with salt and pepper.
3. Bake for about 15 minutes until the eggs are cooked.
4. Squeeze over some lemon juice, scatter over the parsley and enjoy!
5. TIP: Vary up the spices, if you like. Try adding some ground cumin and coriander seed along with the pepper flakes, for a middle-eastern version.

Nutritional Values, estimated per serving: Macros: Protein 13% / Fat 72% / Carbs 16%; Calories: 437 | Total carbs: 20 g | Net carbs: 7 g | Sugar: 2 g | Protein 14 g | Fat: 37 g | Saturated fat: 7 g | Cholesterol: 283 mg | Sodium: 123 mg; Glycemic Load: 2.36

SHAKSHUKA

vegetarian, gluten-free

 SERVES: 2

 PREP TIME: 5 MINUTES

 COOK TIME: 25 MINUTES

5 INGREDIENTS

- 4 medium eggs
- 1 15 oz (450 g) can tomatoes
- 1 onion, peeled and sliced
- 2 oz (60 g) feta, crumbled
- 1 small bunch of parsley, roughly chopped

From the pantry
- 1 tbsp olive oil
- 1 tbsp ras el hanout
- Salt and pepper

METHOD

1. Warm the olive oil in a large frying pan over medium heat, and add the onion with a pinch of salt. Fry until softened and starting to color at the edges.
2. Add the ras el hanout, fry for another 2 minutes, then add the tomatoes.
3. Cook for about 15-20 minutes, until the tomato sauce has thickened slightly. Season to taste.
4. Make 4 little dips in the sauce, and crack the eggs into each one. Continue cooking for about 6-8 minutes, until the egg whites are cooked, and the yolks still running.
5. Scatter with the feta cheese and parsley, and enjoy!
6. TIP: If you like it spicy, add a tbsp of harissa paste along with the spices!

Nutritional Values, estimated per serving: Macros: Protein 22% / Fat 59% / Carbs 19%; Calories: 335 | Total carbs: 18 g | Net carbs: 11 g | Sugar: 9 g | Protein 19 g | Fat: 22 g | Saturated fat: 8 g | Cholesterol: 353 mg | Sodium: 940 mg; Glycemic Load: 5.94

SUPER GREEN SMOOTHIE

vegan, gluten-free, lactose-free

 SERVES: 2

 PREP TIME: 5 MINUTES

 COOK TIME: 0 MINUTES

5 INGREDIENTS

- 2 cups (60 g) of raw spinach
- 1 small cucumber, cut into chunks
- 1 cup (230 g) Greek yogurt
- 2 tbsp peanut butter
- 1 thumb sized piece of ginger, peeled and diced

METHOD

1. Put all the ingredients into a blender and blend until very smooth.
2. Pour into two glasses, and enjoy!
3. TIP: If you want a super-smooth version, process through a juicer instead. But be warned - that way you will miss out on lots of healthful fiber!

Nutritional Values, estimated per serving: Macros: Protein 19% / Fat 53% / Carbs 27%; Calories: 233 | Total carbs: 16 g | Net carbs: 14 g | Sugar: 12 g | Protein: 12 g | Fat: 15 g | Saturated fat: 6 g | Cholesterol: 24 mg | Sodium: 125 mg; Glycemic Load: 2.65

EGGS FLORENTINE
vegetarian

 SERVES: 2

 PREP TIME: 10 MINUTES

 COOK TIME: 10 MINUTES

5 INGREDIENTS

- 2 small whole grain English muffins, split open
- 4 medium eggs and 1 yolk
- 4 cups (120 g) spinach, washed
- ½ lemon, zest and juice
- 2 tbsp butter, melted

From the pantry

- 2 tbsp olive oil
- A dash of vinegar
- Salt and pepper

METHOD

1. Put the spinach in a pan with a pinch of salt, and set over medium heat until wilted, just a couple of minutes. Squeeze as much liquid as possible out of it, then add the lemon zest to it, and set aside.
2. Mix the butter and olive oil together, and pour onto the egg yolk drop by drop, whisking constantly, until an emulsion forms, to make a Hollandaise sauce. Add the lemon juice and season to taste.
3. Bring a pan of water to a boil and add a dash of vinegar. Crack the eggs into the hot water and poach for 3-4 minutes, until the whites are set.
4. Meanwhile, toast the muffins, then top with the spinach.
5. Set one poached egg on top of each muffin half, and spoon over the Hollandaise sauce.
6. TIP: You can make Eggs Benedict in the same way, by simply replacing the spinach with ham!

Nutritional Values, estimated per serving: Macros: Protein 15% / Fat 60% / Carbs 25%; Calories: 546 | Total carbs: 35 g | Net carbs: 31 g | Sugar: 1 g | Protein 20 g | Fat: 37 g | Saturated fat: 13 g | Cholesterol: 450 mg | Sodium: 609 mg; Glycemic Load: 13.38

NOODLE BREAKFAST BROTH
vegetarian, gluten-free, lactose-free

 SERVES: 2

 PREP TIME: 5 MINUTES

 COOK TIME: 10 MINUTES

5 INGREDIENTS

- 2 baby bok choy, halved along their length
- 2 medium eggs
- ½ lb (225 g) konjac noodles (shirataki noodles), well rinsed
- 1 carrot, shredded
- 6 cups (1.5 liters) flavorful broth, either meat or vegetarian, as you like

From the pantry

- 1 tbsp soy sauce

METHOD

1. Bring a pan of water to a boil, and cook the eggs for about 8-10 minutes, until the whites are set and the yolk is jammy. Peel, and halve.
2. Dry fry the konjac noodles for about 2 minutes, to improve their texture.
3. Heat the broth until boiling, then add the soy sauce, carrots, bok choy and the konjac noodles. Cook for just 2-3 minutes, until the vegetables soften.
4. Ladle into the serving bowls, and top with the halved boiled eggs.
5. TIP: Top with condiments of your choice! Chili sauce, ginger, scallions, etc. are all very nice with this dish!

Nutritional Values, estimated per serving: Macros: Protein 41% / Fat 22% / Carbs 36%; Calories: 240 | Total carbs: 25 g | Net carbs: 18 g | Sugar: 11 g | Protein 28 g | Fat: 6 g | Saturated fat: 2 g | Cholesterol: 164 mg | Sodium: 1222 mg; Glycemic Load: 7.21

CHAPTER 2
SALADS AND SOUPS

SPANISH GAZPACHO

vegan, lactose-free, gluten-free

 SERVES: 6, AS LUNCH OR APPETIZER

 PREP TIME: 15 MINUTES

 COOK TIME: 0 MINUTES

 CHILL TIME: 2 HOURS

5 INGREDIENTS

- 3 lb (1.4 kg) ripe tomatoes, roughly chopped, juices retained
- 1 small cucumber, peeled and deseeded
- 1 small red onion, peeled and roughly chopped
- 1 green bell pepper, roughly chopped
- 1 red bell pepper, roughly chopped

From the pantry
- ½ cup (120 ml) extra virgin olive oil
- 2 tbsp vinegar
- 1 ½ tsp salt

METHOD

1. Keep back about 1 quarter of the cucumber, bell peppers and onion for a garnish.
2. Put all the other ingredients into a blender and blend until very smooth.
3. Add more salt and pepper to taste.
4. Chill for at least two hours, or overnight, until cold.
5. Dice the remaining cucumber, bell peppers and onion and scatter over as a garnish. Enjoy!
6. TIP: Garlic lovers can add a few cloves of raw garlic to the mix as well!

Nutritional Values, estimated per serving: Macros: Protein 3% / Fat 75% / Carbs 22%; Calories: 221 | Total carbs: 13 g | Net carbs: 9 g | Sugar: 8 g | Protein 3 g | Fat: 19 g | Saturated fat: 3 g | Cholesterol: 0 mg | Sodium: 596 mg; Glycemic Load: 3.91

CELERIAC APPLE SOUP

gluten-free, lactose-free

 SERVES: 4 AS AN APPETIZER

 PREP TIME: 15 MINUTES

 COOK TIME: 30 MINUTES

5 INGREDIENTS

- 1 small celeriac, peeled and diced (about 1 ½ lb, 680 g)
- 1 green apple, peeled and diced
- 1 onion
- 1 quart (950 ml) chicken stock
- 2 sprigs of thyme

From the pantry
- 2 tbsp olive oil
- Salt and pepper

METHOD

1. Warm the olive oil in a pan over medium heat and add the onions with half of the thyme leaves and a pinch of salt. Sauté until softened and starting to pick up color.
2. Add the celeriac and the apple, and keep cooking, stirring regularly, until the celeriac is golden brown in places.
3. Tip in the chicken stock and bring to a boil. Turn the heat down to a simmer and cook until the celeriac is soft, about 15 minutes.
4. Blend until smooth, season to taste, then pour into the serving bowls.
5. Garnish with the remaining thyme sprigs, and enjoy!
6. TIP: If you can get a celeriac with some leaves and stems attached, try using a little of the celery leaf as an extra garnish!

Nutritional Values, estimated per serving: Macros: Protein 13% / Fat 35% / Carbs 51%; Calories: 263 | Total carbs: 35 g | Net carbs: 30 g | Sugar: 12 g | Protein: 10 g | Fat: 10 g | Saturated fat: 2 g | Cholesterol: 8 mg | Sodium: 837 mg; Glycemic Load: 5.83

ASPARAGUS SPINACH SOUP

gluten-free, lactose-free

 SERVES: 4

 PREP TIME: 10 MINUTES

 COOK TIME: 15 MINUTES

5 INGREDIENTS

- 1 lb (450 g) asparagus, cut into short lengths, woody ends trimmed away
- 10 oz (280 g) spinach
- 3 ½ cups (875 ml) chicken stock
- 2 leeks, rough green ends trimmed away, chopped
- 2 lemons, zested and juiced

From the pantry
- 2 tbsp olive oil
- Salt and pepper

METHOD

1. Heat the olive oil in a large saucepan over medium heat, add the leek and 1 tsp salt. Fry over medium heat for about 5 minutes, stirring regularly, until the leek has softened.
2. Add the asparagus, and half the lemon zest, and sauté for another few minutes.
3. Add the stock, bring to the boil, then turn the heat down to a gentle simmer. Cook for about 10 minutes, until the vegetables have cooked right through. Remove a few asparagus tips and reserve for garnish.
4. Add the spinach in large handfuls, stirring as you go. It will wilt very quickly in the hot liquid; just a minute or two.
5. Blend until very smooth, taste, and add more salt and pepper if you need to, plus the lemon juice, tasting as you go. You may not want it all.
6. Ladle into bowls and garnish with the asparagus tip and a pinch of the remaining lemon zest. Enjoy!
7. TIP: For a rich, luxuriant version, try making the Hollandaise Sauce from the Eggs Florentine recipe, and stir in spoonfuls at the table.

Nutritional Values, estimated per serving: Macros: Protein 17% / Fat 43% / Carbs 41%; Calories: 207 | Total carbs: 22 g | Net carbs: 17 g | Sugar: 8 g | Protein 11 g | Fat: 10 g | Saturated fat: 2 g | Cholesterol: 6 mg | Sodium: 949 mg; Glycemic Load: 4.59

ZUCCHINI BASIL SOUP

vegetarian, gluten-free

 SERVES: 2

 PREP TIME: 5 MINUTES

 COOK TIME: 20 MINUTES

5 INGREDIENTS

- 1 lb (450 g) zucchini, sliced
- 2 ½ cups (600 ml) vegetable stock
- ½ cup (115 g) Greek yogurt, plus 4 tbsp to garnish
- 8 cloves of garlic, peeled and sliced
- 1 bunch of basil, leaves and stems separated

From the pantry
- 2 tbsp olive oil
- Salt and pepper

METHOD

1. Put the olive oil and garlic in a pan with a pinch of salt, and set over medium-low heat. Cook for about 3 minutes, until the garlic has softened, but don't let it color.
2. Add the zucchini, and the basil stalks, and carry on cooking until softened, for approximately 8 minutes.
3. Add the stock and bring to a boil. Turn down to a simmer and cook for about 10 minutes until the zucchini is very soft.
4. Stir in ½ cup of Greek yogurt and blend until smooth. Season to taste.
5. Pour into serving bowls and garnish with 1 tbsp yogurt in each bowl, plus the basil leaves. Enjoy!
6. TIP: You can vary up the herbs if you like! Almost any soft green herbs will work well in place of basil: tarragon, parsley, chervil, or a mixture will all be tasty.

Nutritional Values, estimated per serving: Macros: Protein 30% / Fat 51% / Carbs 19%; Calories: 296 | Total carbs: 15 g | Net carbs: 12 g | Sugar: 4 g | Protein 25 g | Fat: 17 g | Saturated fat: 3 g | Cholesterol: 8 mg | Sodium: 1084 mg; Glycemic Load: 7.51

CHILLED CUCUMBER YOGURT SOUP

vegetarian, gluten-free

 SERVES: 2

 PREP TIME: 10 MINUTES

 CHILL TIME: 2 HOURS

5 INGREDIENTS

- 3 large cucumbers, sliced
- 1 lemon, zest and juice
- 1 cup (230 g) Greek yogurt
- 1 clove of garlic, peeled and sliced
- 1 bunch fresh green herbs, e.g. dill, basil, parsley, mint

From the pantry
- 2 tbsp extra virgin olive oil
- Salt and pepper

METHOD

1. Keep one cucumber and a sprig of herbs back for the garnish.
2. Put all the other ingredients in a blender and blend until smooth. Season to taste and chill for at least 2 hours.
3. Dice the reserved cucumber, finely chop the herb sprig, and mix together.
4. Ladle the chilled soup into bowls and scatter over the garnish. Enjoy!
5. TIP: Try toasting some whole spices, like cumin seed, nigella seed, coriander seed, etc in a hot dry pan. Scatter over the cold soup for an Indian flavor.

Nutritional Values, estimated per serving: Macros: Protein 15% / Fat 54% / Carbs 31%; Calories: 265 | Total carbs: 22 g | Net carbs: 18 g | Sugar: 15 g | Protein 10 g | Fat: 16 g | Saturated fat: 3 g | Cholesterol: 7 mg | Sodium: 651 mg; Glycemic Load: 4.46

VICHYSOISSE LEEK SOUP

gluten-free, lactose-free

 SERVES: 4

 PREP TIME: 5 MINUTES

 COOK TIME: 20 MINUTES

 CHILL TIME: 2 HOURS

5 INGREDIENTS

- 6 leeks, rough green ends trimmed away, sliced in thin rounds
- 1 quart (950 ml) chicken stock
- ¾ cup (200 ml) buttermilk
- 2 tbsp crème fraîche or sour cream
- 1 small bunch of chives, finely chopped

From the pantry
- Salt and pepper

METHOD

1. In a large pot, add the leeks with the chicken stock and a pinch of salt.
2. Bring to a boil, then turn down to a simmer and cover with a lid. Cook for approximately 20 minutes, until the leeks are completely cooked.
3. Turn off the heat and allow to cool to lukewarm.
4. Add the buttermilk, then blend until very smooth.
5. Season to taste with extra salt and pepper, then chill until cold.
6. Serve the soup in bowls with a swirl of crème fraîche or sour cream and the chives scattered over.
7. TIP: For a classic version, add a small peeled, diced potato to the pot with the leeks. It will be more filling, but be aware that the net carbs will increase by about 3-4 g!

Nutritional Values, estimated per serving: Macros: Protein 11% / Fat 20% / Carbs 69%; Calories: 121 | Total carbs: 22 g | Net carbs: 20 g | Sugar: 8 g | Protein 4 g | Fat: 3 g | Saturated fat: 2 g | Cholesterol: 1 mg | Sodium: 224 mg; Glycemic Load: 7.12

SPRING PEA SOUP

vegetarian, gluten-free

 SERVES: 2

 PREP TIME: 5 MINUTES

 COOK TIME: 10 MINUTES

5 INGREDIENTS

- 12 oz (340 g) peas, plus a handful of pea shoots
- 6 spears of green asparagus, roughly chopped
- 1 bunch scallions, roughly chopped
- 3 cups (700 ml) vegetable stock
- ½ cup (115 g) Greek yogurt

From the pantry
- 1 tbsp olive oil
- Salt and pepper

METHOD

1. Warm the olive oil in a pan over medium-low heat, and add the scallions with a pinch of salt. Cook for about 5 minutes, until they have softened.
2. Add the peas, saving just a few raw ones for a garnish. Pour in the vegetable stock, bring to a boil, then turn down to a simmer and cook for about 5 minutes.
3. Stir in the Greek yogurt and the mint, and blend until smooth. Season to taste.
4. Pour into serving bowls and garnish with the raw peas and pea shoots. Enjoy!
5. TIP: This soup can be served either hot or chilled. On a warm spring day, try chilling it for two hours, then enjoying it cold, with a squeeze of lemon juice to brighten the flavor.

Nutritional Values, estimated per serving: Macros: Protein 16% / Fat 35% / Carbs 49%; Calories: 204 | Total carbs: 25 g | Net carbs: 19 g | Sugar: 15 g | Protein: 10 g | Fat: 8 g | Saturated fat: 2 g | Cholesterol: 4 mg | Sodium: 892 mg; Glycemic Load: 9.66

CAULIFLOWER SOUP

vegan, gluten-free, lactose-free

 SERVES: 2

 PREP TIME: 10 MINUTES

 COOK TIME: 25 MINUTES

5 INGREDIENTS

- 1 small cauliflower, broken into florets, stalk diced
- 1 onion
- 1 tbsp tahini
- 4 cups (950 ml) vegetable stock
- 1 sprig of parsley, roughly chopped

From the pantry
- 2 tbsp olive oil
- 1 tbsp extra virgin olive oil
- 2 tsp ras el hanout
- Salt and pepper

METHOD

1. Preheat the oven to 400°F. Mix the cauliflower florets with the ras el hanout, salt and pepper, and 1 tbsp of olive oil. Roast for about 20 minutes until golden brown in places.
2. Meanwhile, warm 1 tbsp of olive oil in a pot over medium heat and add the onion and cauliflower stalks with a pinch of salt. Sauté until softened, and just starting to color, about 10 minutes.
3. Add the vegetable stock and bring to a boil. Simmer until the vegetables are very tender, about 15 minutes.
4. Add the tahini and the roasted cauliflower florets, keeping a few back for a garnish.
5. Blend until very smooth, season to taste, then pour into serving bowls.
6. Garnish with the chopped parsley and reserved florets, drizzle over the extra virgin olive oil, and scatter with a pinch of ras el hanout. Enjoy!
7. TIP: Try making this recipe with only 1 cup of the vegetable stock. You'll end up with a much thicker mix, which you can chill, and serve as a healthy cauliflower dip!

Nutritional Values, estimated per serving: Macros: Protein 5% / Fat 72% / Carbs 23%; Calories: 347 | Total carbs: 21 g | Net carbs: 16 g | Sugar: 9 g | Protein: 6 g | Fat: 29 g | Saturated fat: 4 g | Cholesterol: 0 mg | Sodium: 780 mg; Glycemic Load: 7.25

BROCCOLI AND STILTON SOUP

 SERVES: 2

 PREP TIME: 10 MINUTES

 COOK TIME: 50 MINUTES

5 INGREDIENTS

- 1 small broccoli, broken into florets, stalk diced
- 1 onion, peeled and chopped
- 3 oz (85 g) Stilton blue cheese
- 4 cups (950 ml) vegetable stock
- 4 cloves garlic, peeled and chopped

From the pantry
- 1 tbsp olive oil
- Salt and pepper

METHOD

1. Warm the olive oil in a large pan or Dutch oven, and add the onions with a pinch of salt. Sauté for about 5 minutes, until softened, and starting to color.
2. Add the garlic and broccoli, fry for just a few minutes, then pour in the stock.
3. Bring to a boil, then turn down to a simmer. Cook for about 10 minutes, until the broccoli has softened.
4. Add the Stilton, and blend until smooth. Season to taste. You may not need any more salt, but a lot of black pepper is very good here. Enjoy!
5. TIP: Boost the vitamins and the green color with an added handful of fresh spinach, if you like!

Nutritional Values, estimated per serving: Macros: Protein 18% / Fat 52% / Carbs 30%; Calories: 344 | Total carbs:28 g | Net carbs: 19 g | Sugar: 8 g | Protein: 19 g | Fat: 20 g | Saturated fat: 9 g | Cholesterol: 32 mg | Sodium: 746 mg; Glycemic Load: 7.10

ROASTED CHERRY TOMATO SOUP

gluten-free, lactose-free

 SERVES: 4

 PREP TIME: 10 MINUTES

 COOK TIME: 1 HOUR

5 INGREDIENTS

- 2 ½ lb (1.2 kg) cherry tomatoes
- 1 bulb of garlic, cloves separated, unpeeled
- 1 bunch of basil, leaves and stems separated
- 1 tbsp Italian seasoning
- 1 ½ quarts (1.4 liters) chicken stock

From the pantry
- 2 tbsp olive oil
- Salt and pepper

METHOD

1. Preheat the oven to 360°F.
2. Put the tomatoes, garlic, olive oil, Italian seasoning, and basil stems in a roasting pan, season well, and toss together.
3. Roast in the hot oven for about 1 hour, until the cherry tomatoes have split, and browned in places.
4. Squeeze the roast garlic cloves out of their skins, and put into a blender along with the tomatoes and any juices from the pan, and 3 ladles of the chicken stock.
5. Blend until very smooth, then stir in the rest of the stock. Warm through, and serve with the basil leaves as a garnish. Enjoy!
6. TIP: If you use only half the amount of stock, this also makes a great marinara sauce! Swap for vegetable stock if you want it to be vegetarian.

Nutritional Values, estimated per serving: Macros: Protein 12% / Fat 50% / Carbs 38%; Calories: 146 | Total carbs: 15 g | Net carbs: 11 g | Sugar: 9 g | Protein: 6 g | Fat: 8 g | Saturated fat: 1 g | Cholesterol: 8 mg | Sodium: 891 mg; Glycemic Load: 8.91

APPLE AND CELERY SALAD WITH WALNUTS

vegetarian, gluten-free, lactose-free

 SERVES: 2

 PREP TIME: 5 MINUTES

 COOK TIME: 10 MINUTES

5 INGREDIENTS

- 1 green apple, cored and cut into chunks
- 6 ribs of celery, sliced across the grain
- ½ cup (65 g) walnuts, roughly chopped
- 4 large romaine lettuce leaves, cut into pieces
- ½ tbsp mayonnaise

From the pantry
- 1 tsp extra virgin olive oil
- 1 tsp apple cider vinegar
- Salt and pepper

METHOD

1. Mix the mayonnaise, olive oil and vinegar together, and season to taste.
2. Combine the apple, celery, walnuts and lettuce in a large bowl, and pour over the dressing. Toss lightly to coat, and enjoy!
3. TIP: If you prefer to keep it completely plant-based, just omit the mayonnaise, or swap for a vegan one!

Nutritional Values, estimated per serving: Macros: Protein 7% / Fat 65% / Carbs 28%; Calories: 300 | Total carbs: 22 g | Net carbs: 15 g | Sugar: 13 g | Protein: 7 g | Fat: 23 g | Saturated fat: 2 g | Cholesterol: 1 mg | Sodium: 422 mg; Glycemic Load: 5.14

FENNEL, ORANGE, ARUGULA SALAD

vegan, gluten-free, lactose-free

 SERVES: 2

 PREP TIME: 5 MINUTES

 COOK TIME: 0 MINUTES

5 INGREDIENTS

- 1 bulb of fennel, thinly sliced across the grain
- 2 cups (40 g) arugula
- 1 orange, zested, then pith removed, and sliced
- ½ cup (65 g) walnuts, roughly chopped

From the pantry
- 1 tbsp extra virgin olive oil
- Salt and pepper

METHOD

1. Mix the orange zest with the olive oil and season to taste.
2. Toss all the salad ingredients together, and pour over the dressing. Enjoy!
3. TIP: If you want a bit of extra protein, try adding a small can of tuna to the salad as well. Very Sicilian!

Nutritional Values, estimated per serving: Macros: Protein 7% / Fat 68% / Carbs 25%; Calories: 327 | Total carbs: 22 g | Net carbs: 15 g | Sugar: 12 g | Protein: 7 g | Fat: 26 g | Saturated fat: 3 g | Cholesterol: 0 mg | Sodium: 358 mg; Glycemic Load: 8.53

GREEN BEANS WITH ALMONDS

vegan, gluten-free, lactose-free

 SERVES: 2 AS A SIDE

 PREP TIME: 5 MINUTES

 COOK TIME: 5 MINUTES

5 INGREDIENTS

- 2 cups (250 g) French beans
- 2 cloves of garlic, peeled and minced
- 1 lemon, zest and juice
- 2 tbsp sliced almonds

From the pantry
- ¼ tsp ras el hanout
- 1 tbsp extra virgin olive oil
- Salt and pepper

METHOD

1. Bring a pan of salted water to a boil, and cook the beans for about 5 minutes, until no longer squeaky, but still retaining a little crunch. Drain.
2. Meanwhile, toast the almonds in a hot dry pan until fragrant, then add the olive oil, lemon zest, garlic, and ras el hanout, and immediately turn off the heat.
3. Toss the almonds mixture together with the cooked beans, season to taste, and squeeze over the lemon juice. Enjoy!
4. TIP: Serve as a side dish with the pork chop on page 73!

Nutritional Values, estimated per serving: Macros: Protein 6% / Fat 61% / Carbs 33%; Calories: 110 | Total carbs: 11 g | Net carbs: 8 g | Sugar: 5 g | Protein 5 g | Fat: 8 g | Saturated fat: 1 g | Cholesterol: 0 mg | Sodium: 298 mg; Glycemic Load: 2.73

ITALIAN WHITE BEAN SALAD

vegan, gluten-free, lactose-free

 SERVES: 4

 PREP TIME: 5 MINUTES

 COOK TIME: 0 MINUTES

5 INGREDIENTS

- 1 15 oz (450 g) can of white beans, drained and rinsed
- 8 medium tomatoes, quartered
- 2 cups (40 g) arugula
- 1 small red onion, peeled and sliced
- 1 small bunch of parsley, roughly chopped

From the pantry
- 2 tbsp extra virgin olive oil
- ½ tbsp apple cider vinegar
- Salt and pepper

METHOD

1. Mix the olive oil and the vinegar together and season to taste.
2. Put all the other ingredients in a bowl, pour over the dressing and toss together gently. Enjoy!
3. TIP: Some grilled vegetables fit very well with this salad. Try the vegetable kebabs on page 50!

Nutritional Values, estimated per serving: Macros: Protein 14% / Fat 28% / Carbs 57%; Calories: 240 | Total carbs: 35 g | Net carbs: 26 g | Sugar: 8 g | Protein: 11 g | Fat: 8 g | Saturated fat: 1 g | Cholesterol: 0 mg | Sodium: 320 mg; Glycemic Load: 7.6

QUINOA TABBOULEH

vegan, lactose-free, gluten-free

 SERVES: 4

 PREP TIME: 10 MINUTES

 COOK TIME: 0 MINUTES

5 INGREDIENTS

- ½ cup (90 g) quinoa
- 3 large bunches parsley, roughly chopped
- 1 bunch mint, finely chopped
- 4 tomatoes, chopped
- 1 cucumber, chopped

From the pantry
- ¼ cup (60 ml) extra virgin olive oil
- salt and pepper

METHOD

1. Put the quinoa in a dry pan set over medium heat. Cook until smelling toasty, then cover with water, and cook until tender, about 10 minutes. Drain if the water has not all been absorbed.
2. Meanwhile, set the tomatoes and cucumber in a sieve over a bowl, and sprinkle over ½ tsp salt. Leave to rest for 10 minutes, and collect the juices that run from the vegetables.
3. Mix the juices with the olive oil.
4. Combine the cooked quinoa with the vegetables, herbs, and the dressing, toss together, and season to taste. Enjoy
5. TIP: If you want a little more zing, try adding a squeeze of lemon juice to the mix. Or some finely chopped scallions!

Nutritional Values, estimated per serving with only 30ml olive oi: Macros: Protein 10% / Fat 49% / Calories: 199 | Total carbs: 25 g | Net carbs: 19 g | Sugar: 5 g | Protein: 7 g | Fat: 9 g | Saturated fat: 1 g | Cholesterol: 0 mg | Sodium: 343 mg; Glycemic Load: 9.02

SUMMER AVOCADO CHICKEN SALAD

gluten-free, lactose-free

 SERVES: 2

 PREP TIME: 10 MINUTES

 COOK TIME: 15 MINUTES

5 INGREDIENTS

- 2 small chicken breasts (4 oz, 113g each), no skin
- 4 ribs of celery, sliced
- ½ cup (50 g) black olives, pitted
- 1 avocado, skin and stone removed
- 1 small bunch of parsley, roughly chopped

From the pantry
- 2 tbsp extra virgin olive oil
- Salt and pepper

METHOD

1. Put the chicken breasts in a pan and cover with water. Set over a medium heat, and bring to a boil. Poach for about 15 minutes (from the time you turn the flame on), until cooked through and juicy. Leave to cool in the poaching water, then slice.
2. Meanwhile, mash half the avocado with the olive oil until very smooth, and season.
3. Dice the other half of the avocado and mix with the celery, olives, parsley, and chicken.
4. Mix in the avocado-oil dressing and toss to coat. Enjoy!
5. TIP: Save the water that you poach the chicken in. It makes a great light chicken broth for soups!

Nutritional Values, estimated per serving: Macros: Protein 43% / Fat 46% / Carbs 11%; Calories: 588 | Total carbs: 18 g | Net carbs: 6 g | Sugar: 5 g | Protein: 30 g | Fat: 31 g | Saturated fat: 6 g | Cholesterol: 146 mg | Sodium: 742 mg; Glycemic Load: 2.68

FATToUSH

vegan, lactose-free

 SERVES: 4

 PREP TIME: 5 MINUTES

 COOK TIME: 5 MINUTES

5 INGREDIENTS

- 2 small whole grain pita bread, cut into 1-inch squares or triangles
- 10 medium tomatoes, chopped
- 8 leaves of romaine lettuce, chopped
- 1 red onion, peeled and chopped
- 2 green bell peppers, chopped

From the pantry
- 2 tbsp olive oil
- 1 tbsp extra virgin olive oil
- Salt and pepper

METHOD

1. Heat the olive oil in a frying pan and fry the pita squares on both sides until crisp.
2. Mix together the tomatoes, lettuce, red onion and bell peppers with the extra virgin olive oil, and season to taste.
3. Add the pita chips just before serving, so they stay crisp. Enjoy!
4. TIP: Some fresh herbs are good in this salad as well! Try adding a bunch of chopped parsley and mint.

Nutritional Values, estimated per serving: Macros: Protein 7% / Fat 47% / Carbs 46%; Calories: 215 | Total carbs: 27 g | Net carbs: 20 g | Sugar: 11 g | Protein: 6 g | Fat: 11 g | Saturated fat: 2 g | Cholesterol: 0 mg | Sodium: 376 mg; Glycemic Load: 9.61

SPICY CHICKEN SALAD

gluten-free, lactose-free

 SERVES: 2

 PREP TIME: 10 MINUTES

 COOK TIME: 15 MINUTES

5 INGREDIENTS

- 2 small chicken breasts (4 oz, 113g each), no skin
- 2 tbsp cashew nuts, toasted
- 4 scallions, sliced
- 4 mild red chilis, sliced
- 2 shallots, peeled and thinly sliced

From the pantry
- 1 tbsp soy sauce
- 1 tbsp olive oil
- 1 tsp apple cider vinegar

METHOD

1. Put the chicken breasts in a pan and cover with water. Set over a medium heat, and bring to a boil. Poach for about 15 minutes (from the time you turn the flame on), until cooked through and juicy. Leave to cool in the poaching water, then shred roughly.
2. Meanwhile, mix the soy sauce, olive oil, and vinegar together, and season to taste, to make a dressing.
3. Toss the shredded chicken with all the other ingredients and pour over the dressing. Enjoy!
4. TIP: If you like it spicy, don't be afraid to swap the mild chilis for ones that are as hot as you like!

Nutritional Values, estimated per serving: Macros: Protein 39% / Fat 44% / Carbs 17%; Calories: 322 | Total carbs: 15 g | Net carbs: 12 g | Sugar: 7 g | Protein: 31 g | Fat: 16 g | Saturated fat: 3 g | Cholesterol: 53 mg | Sodium: 392 mg; Glycemic Load: 3.25

ToMATo AND LENTiLS SALAD

vegan, gluten-free, lactose-free

 SERVES: 2

 PREP TIME: 10 MINUTES

 COOK TIME: 20 MINUTES

5 INGREDIENTS

- 2 cups (300 g) cherry tomatoes, halved
- 1 cup (210 g) brown lentils
- 1 tbsp ginger, peeled and minced
- 4 scallions, chopped
- 6 small onions or shallots, peeled and cut into wedges

From the pantry

- 1 tbsp olive oil
- 1 tbsp extra virgin olive oil
- Salt and pepper

METHOD

1. Preheat the oven to 400°F. Put the onions into a roasting pan, season, and toss with the olive oil. Roast for about 20 minutes, until softened and sweet. Take out of the oven and add the ginger to the roasting pan, so it mellows a little in the residual heat.
2. Meanwhile, rinse the lentils, put into a pan, and cover with water. Add a pinch of salt and bring to a boil. Simmer until the lentils are tender, about 15-20 minutes. Drain.
3. Mix the warm lentils with the onions, tomatoes, and scallions. Drizzle over the extra virgin olive oil, and season to taste. Enjoy.
4. TIP: You can roast other vegetables along with the onions, if you like. Zucchini and eggplant are particularly good!

Nutritional Values, estimated per serving: Macros: Protein 15% / Fat 28% / Carbs 57%; Calories: 462 | Total carbs: 66 g | Net carbs: 45 g | Sugar: 17 g | Protein: 21 g | Fat: 15 g | Saturated fat: 2 g | Cholesterol: 0 mg | Sodium: 757 mg; Glycemic Load: 13.51

ASIAN BEEF SALAD

gluten-free, lactose-free

 SERVES: 2

 PREP TIME: 10 MINUTES

 COOK TIME: 6 MINUTES

5 INGREDIENTS

- 12 oz (330 g) lean beef steak
- 1 red onion, peeled and sliced
- 2 limes, zest and juice
- 2 cups (300 g) cherry tomatoes, halved
- 2 tbsp roasted nuts, e.g. cashews or peanuts, or a mix

From the pantry

- 1 tsp harissa chili paste
- 2 tbsp olive oil
- 1 tbsp soy sauce

METHOD

1. Set a skillet over high heat. Brush the steak with a little oil and sear on all sides. Cook until done to your liking, (about 3 minutes each side for medium-rare) then remove from the pan and set aside to rest. Deglaze the pan with the juice of 1 lime.
2. Mix the harissa paste with the juices from the pan, the olive oil, juice of remaining half lime, all the zest and the soy sauce. Season to taste.
3. Slice the steak very thinly and mix with all the other ingredients. Pour over the dressing, and serve with the remaining lime cut into wedges, to squeeze over. Enjoy!
4. TIP: Mix in whatever greens you fancy! Thinly sliced lettuce, cabbage, spinach, scallions, or bok choy are all great additions!

Nutritional Values, estimated per serving: Macros: Protein 36% / Fat 53% / Carbs 11%; Calories: 454 | Total carbs: 14 g | Net carbs: 11 g | Sugar: 6 g | Protein: 40 g | Fat: 27 g | Saturated fat: 6 g | Cholesterol: 99 mg | Sodium: 404 mg; Glycemic Load: 8.80

CHAPTER 3
SAUCES AND DIPS

CHIMICHURRI SAUCE

vegan, gluten-free, lactose-free

 SERVES: 4

 PREP TIME: 5 MINUTES

 COOK TIME: 0 MINUTES

5 INGREDIENTS

- 1 large bunch parsley
- 1 bunch cilantro
- 1 lemon, zest and juice
- 1 pinch red pepper flakes
- 1 small red onion, peeled and roughly chopped

From the pantry
- 2 tbsp extra virgin olive oil
- Salt and pepper

METHOD:

1. Put all the ingredients into a food processor, and whizz until very finely chopped.
2. Season to taste, and enjoy!
3. TIP: Chimichurri is excellent with grilled meat. Try it with the kofta kebabs, or the chicken kebab from the meat chapter.

Nutritional Values, estimated per serving: Macros: Protein 6% / Fat 69% / Carbs 25%; Calories: 94 | Total carbs: 7 g | Net carbs: 4 g | Sugar:2 g | Protein: 2 g | Fat: 7 g | Saturated fat: 1 g | Cholesterol: 0 mg | Sodium: 329 mg; Glycemic Load: 3.06

SMOKY ToMATo DIP

Vegan, vegetarian, pescetarian, gluten-free, lactose-free

 SERVES: 4

 PREP TIME: 5 MINUTES

 COOK TIME: 10 MINUTES

5 INGREDIENTS

- 2 small hot red chilis
- 8 medium tomatoes, halved
- 1 small bunch of parsley, finely chopped
- 3 cloves of garlic, peeled and minced
- ½ tsp smoked paprika

From the pantry
- 1 tbsp extra virgin olive oil
- Salt and pepper
- ½ tsp ras el hanout

METHOD:

1. Get a ridged griddle pan really hot. Brush the tomatoes and chilis with a little oil and grill until you have blackened char-lines on all sides. Set aside to cool.
2. When cool enough to handle, dice the tomatoes and chilis, and mix with all the other ingredients. Season to taste, and enjoy!
3. TIP: If you want, try charring an onion on the pan as well, and adding it for a little extra sweetness.

Nutritional Values, estimated per serving: Macros: Protein 9% / Fat 39% / Carbs 52%; Calories: 93 | Total carbs: 14 g | Net carbs: 10 g | Sugar: 8 g | Protein: 3 g | Fat: 4 g | Saturated fat: 1 g | Cholesterol: 0 mg | Sodium: 314 mg; Glycemic Load: 3.63

GREMOLATA

vegan, gluten-free, lactose-free

 SERVES: 4

 PREP TIME: 5 MINUTES

 COOK TIME: 0 MINUTES

5 INGREDIENTS

- 1 large bunch of parsley, finely chopped
- 2 lemons, zest only
- 4 cloves of garlic, peeled and minced

METHOD:

1. Simply mix all the ingredients together, and carry on chopping finely, to amalgamate them a bit more.
2. Can be used to scatter over multiple dishes, to add flavor.
3. TIP: Some people add a minced anchovy or two, for some extra savoriness. Give it a try!

Nutritional Values, estimated per serving: Macros: Protein 21% / Fat 13% / Carbs 73%; Calories: 21 | Total carbs: 5 g | Net carbs: 4 g | Sugar: 1 g | Protein: 1 g | Fat: <1 g | Saturated fat: <1 g | Cholesterol: 0 mg | Sodium: 18 mg; Glycemic Load: 1.64

ROASTED RED PEPPER DIP

vegan, gluten-free, lactose-free

 SERVES: 4

 PREP TIME: 5 MINUTES

 COOK TIME: 20 MINUTES

5 INGREDIENTS

- 4 medium tomatoes
- 2 red bell peppers
- 1 tsp smoked paprika
- ½ tsp ground cumin
- 2 tbsp almonds, toasted

From the pantry
- 1 tbsp extra virgin olive oil
- 1 tsp apple cider vinegar
- Salt and pepper

METHOD:

1. Heat your oven as high as it goes and roast the bell peppers and tomatoes until soft and blackened, about 20 minutes.
2. Leave the peppers and tomatoes to cool until you can touch them. Peel off the skin and discard, but retain any juices in the roasting pan.
3. Blend the cooked bell peppers and the tomatoes with the paprika, cumin, olive oil and vinegar.
4. Season with salt and pepper to taste. Enjoy!
5. TIP: This is a great sauce for grilled leeks, or it can be used to thicken and add smoky flavor to any tomato based sauce.

Nutritional Values, estimated per serving: Macros: Protein 9% / Fat 54% / Carbs 37%; Calories: 99 | Total carbs: 10 g | Net carbs: 6 g | Sugar: 6 g | Protein: 3 g | Fat: 6 g | Saturated fat: 1 g | Cholesterol: 0 mg | Sodium: 300 mg; Glycemic Load: 3.99

TZATZIKI

vegetarian, gluten-free

 SERVES: 4

 PREP TIME: 5 MINUTES

 COOK TIME: 0 MINUTES

5 INGREDIENTS

- 1 cup (230 g) Greek yogurt
- ½ cup (120 g) cucumber, grated
- 2 tbsp chopped herbs, e.g. dill, mint, parsley
- 1 clove of garlic, peeled and minced
- 1 lemon, zest and juice

From the pantry
- 1 tsp extra virgin olive oil
- Salt and pepper

METHOD:

1. Put the cucumber in a sieve over the sink, and squeeze as much water out of it as you can.
2. Mix the cucumber with all the other ingredients except for the lemon juice.
3. Taste, and season with salt and pepper, the extra virgin olive oil, and as much lemon juice as you think it needs. Enjoy!
4. TIP: Try serving with the crispy fish burger on page 65.

Nutritional Values, estimated per serving: Macros: Protein 48% / Fat 21% / Carbs 30%; Calories: 61 | Total carbs: 5 g | Net carbs: 5 g | Sugar: 3 g | Protein: 8 g | Fat: 2 g | Saturated fat: <1 g | Cholesterol: 4 mg | Sodium: 318 mg; Glycemic Load: 1.12

WHITE BEAN HUMMUS

Vegan, vegetarian, pescetarian, gluten-free, lactose-free

 SERVES: 4

 PREP TIME: 5 MINUTES

 COOK TIME: 0 MINUTES

5 INGREDIENTS

- 1 15 oz (450 g) can white cannellini beans, drained and rinsed
- 2 cloves of garlic, peeled and sliced
- 1 lemon, zest and juice
- 1 tsp sweet paprika
- 2 tbsp flax seeds, toasted

From the pantry
- 4 tbsp extra virgin olive oil
- Salt and pepper

METHOD:

1. Put the beans, garlic, lemon zest, lemon juice and 3 tbsp of the olive oil into a food processor. Blend until very smooth, and season to taste.
2. Mix the paprika with the rest of the olive oil.
3. Stir the flax seed into the hummus, and drizzle with the paprika oil. Enjoy!
4. TIP: You can use the same method with almost any type of beans, seeds and spices! Try black beans with pumpkin seeds and cumin!

Nutritional Values, estimated per serving: Macros: Protein 11% / Fat 52% / Carbs 37%; Calories: 273 | Total carbs: 25 g | Net carbs: 19 g | Sugar: 1 g | Protein: 9 g | Fat: 16 g | Saturated fat: 2 g | Cholesterol: 0 mg | Sodium: 588 mg; Glycemic Load: 5.41

BEETROOT DIP

vegetarian, gluten-free

 SERVES: 6

 PREP TIME: 5 MINUTES

 COOK TIME: 0 MINUTES

5 INGREDIENTS

- 4 beets, peeled and grated
- 2 cups (460 g) of thick Greek yogurt
- 1 tbsp tahini
- 2 cloves of garlic, crushed
- 1 lemon, zest and juice

From the pantry
- 2 tbsp extra virgin olive oil
- Salt and pepper

METHOD:

1. Put all the ingredients except the lemon juice and salt and pepper into the bowl of a food processor. Process until very smooth.
2. Season to taste, adding as much lemon juice as you like. Enjoy!
3. TIP: Try adding some nuts to the mix for a more filling and protein-rich result!

Nutritional Values, estimated per serving: Macros: Protein 31% / Fat 41% / Carbs 28%; Calories: 136 | Total carbs: 10 g | Net carbs: 8 g | Sugar: 7 g | Protein: 11 g | Fat: 6 g | Saturated fat: 1 g | Cholesterol: 5 mg | Sodium: 467 mg; Glycemic Load: 5.66

MUHAMMARA

vegan, lactose-free

 SERVES: 6

 PREP TIME: 10 MINUTES

 COOK TIME: 20 MINUTES

5 INGREDIENTS

- 2 red bell peppers
- 1/2 lb (225 g) toasted walnuts, shelled
- 2 garlic cloves
- 1 small slice of stale white country bread
- 2 tbsp pomegranate molasses

From the pantry
- 3 tbsp extra virgin olive oil
- Salt and pepper

METHOD

1. Heat your oven as high as it goes and roast the bell peppers until soft and blackened, about 20 minutes
2. Leave the peppers to cool until you can touch them, then peel off the skin and discard. Roughly chop the cooked bell peppers.
3. Meanwhile, tear the bread into pieces and pour the pomegranate molasses over it.
4. Blend the cooked bell peppers and the bread with the walnuts, garlic cloves, and the olive oil.
5. Season with salt and pepper to taste. Enjoy!
6. TIP: Serve with vegetable crudités to dip in.

Nutritional Values, estimated per serving: Macros: Protein 7% / Fat 79% / Carbs 14%; Calories: 339 | Total carbs: 12 g | Net carbs: 8 g | Sugar: 4 g | Protein:7 g | Fat: 32 g | Saturated fat: 3 g | Cholesterol: 0 mg | Sodium: 53 mg; Glycemic Load: 3.49

AIOLI

vegetarian, gluten-free, lactose-free

 SERVES: 6

 PREP TIME: 10 MINUTES

 COOK TIME: 0 MINUTES

5 INGREDIENTS

- 1 egg yolk
- 1 small bunch of chives, finely chopped (optional)
- 2 cloves of garlic, peeled and crushed
- ½ a lemon, juice only

From the pantry

- ½ cup (120 ml) olive oil
- Salt and pepper

METHOD:

1. Mix the egg yolk with the garlic, and season.
2. While mixing with an electric whisk, pour the olive oil in, very slowly.
3. Continue whisking as you see the emulsion forming.
4. Stir in the chives, and squeeze in the lemon juice to taste. Enjoy!
5. TIP: Some people like to make it with extra virgin olive oil, for a richer flavor and deeper color!

Nutritional Values, estimated per serving: Macros: Protein 1% / Fat 97% / Carbs 1%; Calories: 171 | Total carbs: 1 g | Net carbs: 1 g | Sugar: <1 g | Protein: 1 g | Fat: 19 g | Saturated fat: 3 g | Cholesterol: 31 mg | Sodium: 196 mg; Glycemic Load: 0.22

SCALLION SAUCE

vegan, lactose-free

 SERVES: 6

 PREP TIME: 5 MINUTES

 COOK TIME: 5 MINUTES

5 INGREDIENTS

- 1 bunch of scallions, roughly chopped
- 2 cloves of garlic, peeled and minced
- 4 small green chili peppers, shredded
- 2 tbsp ginger, peeled and minced
- 2 tbsp sesame seeds

From the pantry

- ½ cup (120 ml) vegetable oil
- 1 tbsp soy sauce
- Salt and pepper

METHOD:

1. Put the scallions, garlic, chilis, ginger and sesame seeds into a heat proof bowl.
2. Heat the oil to 350°F (hot enough for a crumb of bread to sizzle and immediately turn brown.)
3. Pour the hot oil onto the scallion mix. Be careful, it will sizzle and spit a little!
4. Leave to cool to room temperature, then add the soy sauce, and season to taste. Enjoy!
5. TIP: If you don't like it so spicy, just reduce or omit the chili peppers - it's still delicious without!

Nutritional Values, estimated per serving: Macros: Protein 8% / Fat 80% / Carbs 12%; Calories: 216 | Total carbs: 7 g | Net carbs: 5 g | Sugar: 2 g | Protein: 5 g | Fat: 20 g | Saturated fat: 2g | Cholesterol: 0 mg | Sodium: 285 mg; Glycemic Load: 1.63

CHAPTER 4
VEGETARIAN

GADO GADO

vegetarian, gluten-free, lactose-free

 SERVES: 2

 PREP TIME: 5 MINUTES

 COOK TIME: 10 MINUTES

5 INGREDIENTS

- 2 tbsp spicy peanut sauce (e.g. Satay)
- 2 medium eggs
- 2 cups (260 g) of bean sprouts
- 2 tbsp scallion sauce (page 44)
- Mixed veggies of choice, e,g, green beans, carrots, spinach

From the pantry
- 1 tbsp soy sauce

METHOD:

1. Steam the vegetables for a few minutes, until softened but still slightly crunchy.
2. Boil the eggs for 10 minutes, then run under cold water, peel and quarter.
3. Split the vegetables, eggs, and bean sprouts between 2 serving plates, and drizzle over the scallion sauce and the soy sauce.
4. Serve with the peanut sauce on the side, and enjoy!
5. TIP: Add some fried tofu for extra protein, if you like, and mix up the veggies! Part of the joy of Gado Gado is throwing in whatever you have to hand.

Nutritional Values, estimated per serving: Macros: Protein 24% / Fat 41% / Carbs 35%; Calories: 232 | Total carbs: 22 g | Net carbs: 18 g | Sugar: 10 g | Protein: 18 g | Fat: 11 g | Saturated fat: 2 g | Cholesterol: 164 mg | Sodium: 1357 mg; Glycemic Load: 6.93

BEET BURGERS

vegan, gluten-free, lactose-free

 MAKES: 4 BURGER PATTIES

 PREP TIME: 10 MINUTES

 COOK TIME: 20 MINUTES

5 INGREDIENTS

- 2 small beets, peeled and grated
- ½ cup (50 g) rolled oats
- ½ cup (40 g) walnuts
- ½ cup (100 g) cooked brown rice
- 1 onion, peeled and diced

From the pantry
- 1 tbsp tomato paste
- 1 tbsp Italian seasoning
- 2 tbsp olive oil for frying
- 1 tbsp soy sauce

METHOD:

1. Heat 1 tbsp olive oil in a skillet over medium heat, and fry the onion for about 5 minutes, until translucent.
2. Add the tomato paste, soy sauce, and Italian seasoning and fry for about another 2 minutes, then add the beets. Cook for just 2 minutes, then turn off the heat and set aside to cool.
3. Put the oats, walnuts, and rice into a food processor, and blitz until you have a coarse powder. Add the beet mixture as well, and pulse a few more times, until the mix is homogenous, but still coarse-textured.
4. Shape into 4 burger patties, pressing together well.
5. Heat the other tbsp of olive oil in the skillet, over medium heat, and fry the patties for about 5 minutes each side, turning carefully half way through.
6. Serve hot, and enjoy!
7. TIP: These are lovely just as they are, but you can use them as a patty in a complete burger with a low-carb bun!

Nutritional Values, estimated per serving: Macros: Protein 9% / Fat 46% / Carbs 46%; Calories: 284 | Total carbs: 32 g | Net carbs: 26 g | Sugar: 8 g | Protein: 7 g | Fat: 15 g | Saturated fat: 2 g | Cholesterol: 0 mg | Sodium: 325 mg; Glycemic Load: 12.86

SPAGHETTI WITH FRESH BEANS

vegetarian, lactose-free

 SERVES: 2

 PREP TIME: 5 MINUTES

COOK TIME: 10 MINUTES

5 INGREDIENTS

- 1 cup (150 g) of cherry tomatoes, halved
- 1 cup (160 g) of fresh edamame or fava beans
- 1 small bunch of chives, finely chopped
- 4 oz (110 g) wholewheat spaghetti
- 2 oz (60 g) parmesan, grated

From the pantry
- 2 tbsp extra virgin olive oil
- Salt and pepper

METHOD:

1. Cook the spaghetti according to packet instructions. When the pasta has about 4 minutes left to cook, add the fresh beans to the pot. Drain, reserving ¼ cup of the cooking water.
2. Mix the reserved hot cooking water with the parmesan and olive oil, to make a loose sauce.
3. Toss the spaghetti in the sauce, along with the beans, chives, and tomatoes. Season to taste, and enjoy!
4. TIP: Using pasta cooking water like this is a great way to loosen up any pasta sauce that is a little too thick.

Nutritional Values, estimated per serving: Macros: Protein 18% / Fat 42% / Carbs 40%; Calories: 545 | Total carbs: 57 g | Net carbs: 47 g | Sugar: 4 g | Protein: 26 g | Fat: 26 g | Saturated fat: 7 g | Cholesterol: 24 mg | Sodium: 815 mg; Glycemic Load: 13.98

ASPARAGUS CARBONARA

lactose-free

 SERVES: 2

 PREP TIME: 5 MINUTES

 COOK TIME: 10 MINUTES

5 INGREDIENTS

- 4 oz (110 g) wholewheat pasta
- 12 oz (330 g) asparagus, cut into short lengths
- 1 egg and 2 yolks
- 2 oz (60 g) bacon or pancetta, diced (Optional, for non-vegetarians)
- 2 oz (60 g) parmesan, grated

From the pantry
- 1 tbsp olive oil
- Salt and pepper

METHOD:

1. Cook the spaghetti according to packet instructions. When the pasta has about 45 minutes left to cook, add the asparagus to the pot. Drain, reserving ¼ cup (~60 ml) of the cooking water.
2. Mix the parmesan with the egg and egg yolks.
3. Meanwhile, fry the bacon in the olive oil, over medium heat, until the fat has rendered and the bacon is starting to crisp in places. Remove with a slotted spoon.
4. Tip the cooking water into the skillet, and stir rapidly. Then pour the liquid into the egg mixture and combine.
5. Add the egg sauce to the cooked pasta and asparagus and stir to mix, so that each strand of spaghetti is coated in the silky sauce. Season to taste.
6. Toss in the bacon, if using, and enjoy!
7. TIP: For an ultra low-carb version, skip the spaghetti and use konjac noodles or zoodles instead!

Nutritional Values, estimated per serving: Macros: Protein 18% / Fat 49% / Carbs 33%; Calories: 614 | Total carbs: 54 g | Net carbs: 46 g | Sugar: 4 g | Protein: 29 g | Fat: 33 g | Saturated fat: 12 g | Cholesterol: 309 mg | Sodium: 766 mg; Glycemic Load: 13.03

VIETNAMESE SUMMER ROLLS

vegan, lactose-free

 SERVES: 2 (6 ROLLS)

 PREP TIME: 15 MINUTES

 COOK TIME: 0 MINUTES

5 INGREDIENTS

- 6 sheets of low-carb rice paper (keto spring roll wrappers)
- 1 carrot, peeled and cut into matchsticks
- ½ a small cucumber, seeded and cut into matchsticks
- 1 cup (75g) red cabbage, very thinly sliced
- ½ red bell pepper, cut into matchsticks

From the pantry
- 2 tbsp soy sauce
- 1 tbsp harissa chili paste

METHOD:

1. Soak 1 sheet of rice paper in water for 20-30 seconds, until pliable, but not soggy. Put it on a clean surface, and put about one sixth of the vegetables on the lower third.
2. Fold over the long side closest to you, followed by the short edges, then roll up. Repeat with the other 5 pieces of rice paper.
3. Whisk the soy sauce and chili paste together, to make a dipping sauce.
4. Cut the summer rolls in half, and serve with the sauce on the side. Enjoy!
5. TIP: If you want to boost the protein content, try adding a little shredded tofu to the filling, or mix some peanut butter into the dipping sauce. And for an ultra low-carb version, try wrapping in nori seaweed sheets instead!

Nutritional Values, estimated per serving: Macros: Protein 11% / Fat 4% / Carbs 85%; Calories: 129 | Total carbs: 27 g | Net carbs: 22 g | Sugar: 7 g | Protein: 4 g | Fat: 1 g | Saturated fat: <1 g | Cholesterol: 0 mg | Sodium: 725 mg; Glycemic Load: 6.31

RED LENTIL DHAL

vegan, gluten-free, lactose-free

 SERVES: 4

 PREP TIME: 10 MINUTES

 COOK TIME: 25 MINUTES

5 INGREDIENTS

- 2 cups (350g) red lentils
- 1 large bunch of cilantro, roughly chopped
- 4 onions
- 6 tbsp fresh ginger, peeled and minced
- 8 cloves of garlic, peeled and minced

From the pantry
- 1 tbsp vegetable oil
- 2 tbsp garam masala
- Salt and pepper

METHOD:

1. Heat the oil in a large pan over medium heat, and add the onions with a pinch of salt. Fry for about 8-10 minutes, until softened and starting to color.
2. Add the ginger, garlic, and garam masala and fry for another 2 minutes.
3. Add the lentils, stir so everything is mixed well, then pour in enough water to just cover the lentils.
4. Cook for about 15 minutes, stirring frequently, and topping up the water if you need to, until the lentils have collapsed to form a thick porridge.
5. Season to taste, scatter over generous handfuls of cilantro, and enjoy!
6. TIP: If you like it spicy, add a few chopped red chilis to the pot, along with the ginger!

Nutritional Values, estimated per serving: Macros: Protein 20% / Fat 13% / Carbs 67%; Calories: 321 | Total carbs: 54 g | Net carbs: 35 g | Sugar: 8 g | Protein: 19 g | Fat: 5 g | Saturated fat: 1 g | Cholesterol: 0 mg | Sodium: 746 mg; Glycemic Load: 14.23

CAULIFLOWER PICATA

vegan, gluten-free, lactose-free

 SERVES: 2

 PREP TIME: 5 MINUTES

 COOK TIME: 10 MINUTES

5 INGREDIENTS

- 2 cauliflower "steaks" (fat slices through the stem, from a small cauliflower)
- 1 lemon, zest and juice
- 2 tbsp capers
- 2 shallots, peeled and minced
- 1 tbsp wholewheat flour

From the pantry
- 2 tbsp olive oil
- 1 tbsp extra virgin olive oil
- Salt and pepper

METHOD:

1. Season the flour with salt and pepper, and sprinkle over both sides of each cauliflower "steak".
2. Heat the olive oil in a large skillet over medium-high heat, and add the cauliflower. Fry for about 5 minutes each side, until golden brown and crunchy, then lift out onto warmed serving plates.
3. Add the shallots to the pan, and turn the heat down a little. Fry until softened, then add the capers, lemon zest, and extra virgin olive oil, and squeeze in half the lemon juice. Stir to deglaze the pan, then season to taste and drizzle over the cauliflower steaks.
4. Serve with the other half of the lemon, cut into wedges, and enjoy!
5. TIP: Try serving with hummus on the side, and/or a fresh green salad!

Nutritional Values, estimated per serving: Macros: Protein 6% / Fat 68% / Carbs 26%; Calories: 274 | Total carbs: 20 g | Net carbs: 14 g | Sugar: 7 g | Protein: 6 g | Fat: 21 g | Saturated fat: 3 g | Cholesterol: 0 mg | Sodium: 861 mg; Glycemic Load: 5.54

ZOODLES WITH VEGAN BOLOGNESE

vegan, gluten-free, lactose-free

 SERVES: 4

 PREP TIME: 15 MINUTES

 COOK TIME: 20 MINUTES

5 INGREDIENTS

- 1 portion roasted red pepper dip from page 41
- 2 cups (160g) walnuts, chopped into rubble
- 4 zucchini, spiralized into zoodles
- 2 onions, peeled and diced
- 3 carrots, finely diced

From the pantry
- 1 tbsp olive oil
- 1 tbsp extra virgin olive oil
- Salt and pepper

METHOD:

1. Heat the olive oil in a pan over medium heat and sauté the onion with a pinch of salt until softened and starting to color, about 8-10 minutes.
2. Add the carrots and walnuts and carry on cooking for another 5 minutes.
3. Add the tomato sauce, bring to a boil, and simmer for just a few minutes, until the sauce thickens and comes together. Season to taste.
4. Meanwhile, toss the zoodles with the extra virgin olive oil, and divide between 4 serving plates.
5. Top with the vegan ragu, and enjoy!
6. TIP: Fresh basil leaves make a great summery garnish for this dish!

Nutritional Values, estimated per serving: Macros: Protein 8% / Fat 65% / Carbs 27%; Calories: 651 | Total carbs: 47 g | Net carbs: 33 g | Sugar: 26 g | Protein: 16 g | Fat: 41 g | Saturated fat: 5 g | Cholesterol: 0 mg | Sodium: 696 mg; Glycemic Load: 11.64

MIXED GREENS APPLE SALAD

vegetarian, gluten-free

SERVES: 2

PREP TIME: 5 MINUTES

COOK TIME: 0 MINUTES

5 INGREDIENTS

- 4 cups (120 g) of spring mix or baby-leaf spinach
- 1 tbsp dried cranberries
- 1 cup (80 g) walnuts, toasted
- 1 apple, cored and sliced
- 4 oz (110 g) feta cheese, crumbled

From the pantry

- 2 tbsp extra virgin olive oil
- Salt and pepper

METHOD:

1. Toss all the ingredients together, and drizzle over the olive oil.
2. Season to taste, and enjoy!
3. TIP: Try swapping the feta for some blue cheese, for an interesting variation!

Nutritional Values, estimated per serving: Macros: Protein 10% / Fat 75% / Carbs 15%; Calories: 669 | Total carbs: 27 g | Net carbs: 20 g | Sugar: 16 g | Protein: 18 g | Fat: 59 g | Saturated fat: 13 g | Cholesterol: 50 mg | Sodium: 860 mg; Glycemic Load: 6.22

GRILLED VEGETABLE SKEWERS

vegan, gluten-free, lactose-free

SERVES: 4 (8 SKEWERS)

PREP TIME: 5 MINUTES

COOK TIME: 10 MINUTES

5 INGREDIENTS

- 1 zucchini, cut into fat half-moons
- 1 red onion, cut into wedges
- 1 yellow bell pepper, cut into chunks
- 1 cup (150 g) cherry tomatoes
- ½ lb (225 g) small cremini or button mushrooms

From the pantry

- 1 tbsp olive oil
- Salt and pepper

METHOD:

1. Put all the vegetables into a large bowl, season well, and add the olive oil. Toss together to coat well.
2. Thread the vegetables onto 8 skewers, alternating types and colors.
3. Grill for about 10 minutes, turning several times, until lightly charred and cooked. Enjoy!
4. TIP: These are great to serve at a barbecue. Make sure to stick to low-carb sides!

Nutritional Values, estimated per serving: Macros: Protein 11% / Fat 41% / Carbs 48%; Calories: 86 | Total carbs: 11 g | Net carbs: 8 g | Sugar: 5 g | Protein: 4 g | Fat: 4 g | Saturated fat: 1 g | Cholesterol: 0 mg | Sodium: 304 mg; Glycemic Load: 3.79

GRIDDLED ZUCHINI WITH FETA CHEESE

Vegan, vegetarian, pescetarian, gluten-free, lactose-free

 SERVES: 2

 PREP TIME: 5 MINUTES

 COOK TIME: 5 MINUTES

5 INGREDIENTS

- 2 zucchini, cut into ¼ inch thick rounds
- 4 oz (113 g) feta cheese, sliced
- 2 cloves of garlic, peeled and thinly sliced
- 1 lemon, zest and juice
- 2 cups (40 g) arugula

From the pantry
- 1 tbsp olive oil
- 1 tbsp extra virgin olive oil
- ¼ tsp Italian seasoning
- Salt and pepper

METHOD:

1. Toss the zucchini with the olive oil and Italian seasoning, and season with salt and pepper.
2. On a ridged griddle pan over high heat, grill the zucchini on both sides, until you see golden brown lines, about 2 minutes each side.
3. Toss the zucchini together with the garlic, lemon zest and juice, and leave for a few minutes.
4. Add the feta cheese and rucola, and drizzle over the extra virgin olive oil. Enjoy!
5. TIP: Any griddled vegetables work well here. Try it with eggplant, bell peppers, onions, or a mixture!

Nutritional Values, estimated per serving: Macros: Protein 14% / Fat 73% / Carbs 13%; Calories: 318 | Total carbs: 12 g | Net carbs: 9 g | Sugar: 8 g | Protein: 11 g | Fat: 26 g | Saturated fat: 11 g | Cholesterol: 50 mg | Sodium: 858 mg; Glycemic Load: 2.85

GRILLED TOFU WITH SOBA NOODLES

vegan, lactose-free

 SERVES: 4

 PREP TIME: 5 MINUTES

 COOK TIME: 15 MINUTES

5 INGREDIENTS

- 4 oz (113 g)soba noodles
- ½ cup (80g) of peanuts, toasted
- 12 oz (330 g) extra firm tofu, drained and pressed, cut into slices
- 4 cups (160 g) of spinach
- 1 cup (50 g) fresh shiitake mushrooms, sliced

From the pantry
- 2 tbsp vegetable oil
- 1 tbsp soy sauce
- Salt and pepper

METHOD:

1. Cook the soba noodles according to packet instructions, drain and tip into a large bowl. Add the spinach, so it wilts in the residual heat.
2. Meanwhile, heat 1 tbsp oil in a skillet over medium heat, and fry the mushrooms for about 8-10 minutes, until colored in places and cooked through. Add the soy sauce, let it bubble for a moment, then tip the whole lot into the bowl with the noodles.
3. Heat the other tbsp of oil in the same skillet, and fry the tofu slices for about 3 minutes each side, until golden brown.
4. Add the peanuts to the bowl, toss everything together and split between 4 serving bowls.
5. Top with the tofu slices, and enjoy!
6. TIP: Mix in some extra vegetables, if you like. Grilled eggplant in particular is a great addition here.

Nutritional Values, estimated per serving: Macros: Protein 17% / Fat 49% / Carbs 33%; Calories: 365 | Total carbs: 32 g | Net carbs: 29 g | Sugar: 3 g | Protein: 19 g | Fat: 21 g | Saturated fat: 3 g | Cholesterol: 0 mg | Sodium: 388 mg; Glycemic Load: 10.06

MISO GRILLED EGGPLANT

vegan, lactose-free

 SERVES: 2

 PREP TIME: 10 MINUTES

 COOK TIME: 20 MINUTES

5 INGREDIENTS

- 2 medium eggplant, sliced lengthwise, scored in a criss-cross pattern
- 2 tsp light miso paste
- 2 tbsp mirin or rice wine
- 1 tbsp sesame seeds
- 2 scallions, sliced

From the pantry
- 1 tsp vegetable oil

METHOD:

1. Preheat the grill setting in your oven and set a large skillet over medium-high heat.
2. Brush the cut sides of the eggplant with oil and fry cut-side down, for about 3 minutes until browned. Flip, cover the pan, and cook for another 3 minutes, until the eggplant halves are cooked through, but not collapsing.
3. Meanwhile, whisk the miso and mirin together. Put the cooked eggplants, cut side up, onto a baking tray lined with foil and brush them all generously with the miso mix.
4. Put into the oven and broil/grill for 4-5 minutes, until bubbling on top. Sprinkle with the sesame seeds and scallions, and serve 2 halves per person. Enjoy!
5. TIP: Serve with steamed Asian greens, for a very satisfying and low-carb side!

Nutritional Values, estimated per serving: Macros: Protein 12% / Fat 26% / Carbs 62%; Calories: 275 | Total carbs: 44 g | Net carbs: 24 g | Sugar: 22 g | Protein: 11 g | Fat: 8 g | Saturated fat: 1 g | Cholesterol: 0 mg | Sodium: 1298 mg; Glycemic Load: 6.92

CHICKPEA CURRY

vegan, gluten-free, lactose-free

 SERVES: 4

 PREP TIME: 10 MINUTES

 COOK TIME: 20 MINUTES

5 INGREDIENTS

- 2 15 oz (450 g) cans of chickpeas
- 2 tbsp Thai red curry paste
- 4 zucchini, cut into chunks
- 2 onions, peeled and chopped
- 1 bunch of cilantro, roughly

From the pantry
- 2 tbsp vegetable oil
- 1 tbsp tomato paste
- 1 tbsp garam masala
- Salt and pepper

METHOD:

1. Heat the oil in a wok or large frying pan over medium-high heat and add the onions. Fry for about 5 minutes, until translucent, then add the zucchini.
2. Carry on frying for another 5 minutes, then add the garam masala, tomato paste, and Thai red curry paste. Keep frying briskly for 2 minutes, until fragrant, then add the chickpeas and the liquid in the cans. Top up with a little water, so just covered.
3. Bring to a boil, then turn down to a simmer. Cook for about 8-10 minutes, until the sauce has thickened slightly. Season to taste.
4. Scatter over the cilantro, and enjoy!
5. TIP: Serve with limes on the side, to squeeze over for extra piquancy!

Nutritional Values, estimated per serving: Macros: Protein 14% / Fat 31% / Carbs 54%; Calories: 322 | Total carbs: 45 g | Net carbs: 32 g | Sugar: 10 g | Protein: 14 g | Fat: 12 g | Saturated fat: 2 g | Cholesterol: 0 mg | Sodium: 908 mg; Glycemic Load: 12.37

MUSHROOM SOUP

vegan, gluten-free, lactose-free

 SERVES: 2

 PREP TIME: 10 MINUTES

 COOK TIME: 10 MINUTES

5 INGREDIENTS

- 1 lb (450 g) mixed mushrooms, sliced
- 1 onion, peeled and sliced
- 2 carrots, thinly sliced or chopped
- 1 sprig of thyme, leaves only
- 1 quart of vegetable stock

From the pantry
- 2 tbsp olive oil
- ½ tsp Italian seasoning
- 1 tsp tomato paste
- Salt and pepper

METHOD:

1. Warm the olive oil in a large pan over medium heat, and add the onion with a pinch of salt. Fry until softened and starting to color at the edges, 8-10 minutes.
2. Add the carrots, mushrooms, thyme, tomato paste, and the Italian seasoning. Fry for another 5 minutes, until the mushrooms have caramelized in places.
3. Add the vegetable stock and bring to a boil. Turn the heat down and simmer for about 10 minutes, until the vegetables are cooked.
4. Season to taste, and serve with some extra thyme leaves as a garnish. Enjoy!
5. TIP: For a Hungarian mushroom goulash flavor, try adding a teaspoon of paprika along with the mushrooms!

Nutritional Values, estimated per serving: Macros: Protein 9% / Fat 52% / Carbs 39%; Calories: 244 | Total carbs: 25 g | Net carbs: 20 g | Sugar: 14 g | Protein: 8 g | Fat: 15 g | Saturated fat: 2 g | Cholesterol: 0 mg | Sodium: 1157 mg; Glycemic Load: 9.77

BAKED CHICKPEAS WITH SPINACH

vegan, gluten-free, lactose-free

 SERVES: 4

 PREP TIME: 10 MINUTES

 COOK TIME: 1 HOUR 20 MINUTES

5 INGREDIENTS

- 2 15 oz (450 g) cans of chickpeas
- 6 onions, peeled and sliced
- 2 cups (~80 g) spinach leaves, shredded
- 1 lemon, zest and juice
- 1 pinch of red pepper flakes

From the pantry
- 2 tbsp olive oil
- Salt and pepper

METHOD:

1. Preheat the oven to 400°F.
2. Put the sliced onions in a large skillet, with 1 tbsp olive oil and a pinch of salt. Fry over medium heat for about 20 minutes, until golden brown and caramelized. Add the spinach, and cook just a minute or two more, until the spinach has wilted.
3. Meanwhile, rub the remaining tbsp of olive oil over the inside of an ovenproof pot with a lid, or a Dutch oven. Add to it the onions, the chickpeas, along with the liquid in the cans, ½ tsp salt, lemon zest, lemon juice, plenty of freshly ground black pepper, and the red pepper flakes.
4. Pour over enough water to completely cover the contents by about half an inch, put the lid on and put it into the hot oven.
5. Bake for 1 hour, then take the lid off and continue baking for another 15 minutes. Enjoy!
6. TIP: Adding some fresh herbs to the pot is a good addition. Rosemary and thyme are especially good.

Nutritional Values, estimated per serving: Macros: Protein 15% / Fat 37% / Carbs 49%; Calories: 259 | Total carbs: 31 g | Net carbs: 21 g | Sugar: 13 g | Protein: 11 g | Fat: 11 g | Saturated fat: 1 g | Cholesterol: 0 mg | Sodium: 895 mg; Glycemic Load: 16.78

PEPERONATA

vegan, gluten-free, lactose-free

 SERVES: 4

 PREP TIME: 10 MINUTES

 COOK TIME: 20 MINUTES

5 INGREDIENTS

- 2 medium eggplants, sliced into rounds
- 4 medium tomatoes, roughly chopped
- 3 bell peppers, red, yellow, and green
- 2 carrots, cut into batons
- 1 small bunch of parsley, leaves and stems separated, roughly chopped

From the pantry

- 3 tbsp olive oil
- 1 tbsp extra virgin olive oil
- 1 tsp tomato paste
- ¼ tsp Italian seasoning
- Salt and pepper

METHOD:

1. Heat the olive oil in a large frying pan over medium heat and add the eggplants with a pinch of salt. Fry until lightly browned and softened, about 5-6 minutes.
2. Add the bell peppers, carrots, tomato paste, and Italian seasoning and carry on frying for another 4 minutes.
3. Add the tomatoes and the parsley stems, and cover, so that the vegetables steam in their own juices. Cook for about 10 minutes, until the eggplants are completely soft, and the tomatoes have collapsed to form a rough sauce.
4. Stir in the extra virgin olive oil, and season to taste. Scatter over the parsley leaves, and enjoy!
5. TIP: Some people like their peperonata spicy! If that's you, add some sliced chili peppers along with the bell peppers!

Nutritional Values, estimated per serving: Macros: Protein 6% / Fat 50% / Carbs 44%; Calories: 257 | Total carbs: 31 g | Net carbs: 18 g | Sugar: 17 g | Protein: 6 g | Fat: 15 g | Saturated fat: 2 g | Cholesterol: 0 mg | Sodium: 336 mg; Glycemic Load: 7.43

CAULIFLOWER CURRY

vegan, gluten-free, lactose-free

 SERVES: 2

 PREP TIME: 10 MINUTES

 COOK TIME: 20 MINUTES

5 INGREDIENTS

- 1 head of cauliflower, broken into florets, stalk diced
- 1 tbsp turmeric
- 2 onions, peeled and sliced
- 1 tsp ground cumin
- 4 cloves of garlic, peeled and sliced

From the pantry

- 1 tbsp garam masala
- 1 tbsp vegetable oil
- 1 tsp harissa chili paste
- Salt and pepper

METHOD:

1. Heat the olive oil in a large pan over medium heat, and add the onions and cauliflower stalks, with a pinch of salt. Cook until softened and starting to color, about 8-10 minutes.
2. Add the garlic, chili paste, and all of the spices, and cook for 2 minutes.
3. Add the cauliflower florets, and pour in enough water to just cover. Bring to a boil, then turn down to a simmer.
4. Cook for about 10 minutes, until the cauliflower is cooked through. Season to taste, and enjoy!
5. TIP: Serve with brown rice, or a low carb flatbread!

Nutritional Values, estimated per serving: Macros: Protein 11% / Fat 32% / Carbs 56%; Calories: 252 | Total carbs: 39 g | Net carbs: 25 g | Sugar: 13 g | Protein: 11 g | Fat: 9 g | Saturated fat: 1 g | Cholesterol: 0 mg | Sodium: 465 mg; Glycemic Load: 5.67

MOROCCAN EGGPLANT

vegan, gluten-free, lactose-free

 SERVES: 2

 PREP TIME: 10 MINUTES

 COOK TIME: 20 MINUTES

5 INGREDIENTS

- 2 medium eggplants, cut into chunks
- 2 stems of celery, diced
- 8 medium tomatoes, roughly chopped
- 2 cloves of garlic, peeled and sliced
- 1 large leek, roughly chopped

From the pantry

- 1 tbsp ras el hanout
- 1 tbsp olive oil
- 1 tbsp extra virgin olive oil
- 1 tsp apple cider vinegar
- Salt and pepper

METHOD:

1. Heat the olive oil in a large pan over medium-low, and add the leeks with a pinch of salt. Fry gently until softened, but not colored, about 5 minutes.
2. Add the celery, garlic, eggplant and ras el hanout. Keep cooking for another 5 minutes.
3. Add the tomatoes, and turn the heat up a little. Once the tomatoes have released enough juices to make a rough sauce, add the vinegar and bring to a boil.
4. Cook for about 15 minutes, stirring occasionally, until the sauce has reduced and thickened, and the vegetables are cooked through.
5. Stir in the extra virgin olive oil, and season to taste. Enjoy!
6. TIP: Try serving with poached eggs, for breakfast-as-dinner!

Nutritional Values, estimated per serving: Macros: Protein 7% / Fat 36% / Carbs 56%; Calories: 393 | Total carbs: 62 g | Net carbs: 37 g | Sugar: 35 g | Protein: 11 g | Fat: 16 g | Saturated fat: 2 g | Cholesterol: 0 mg | Sodium: 370 mg; Glycemic Load: 9.63

BUDDHA BOWL

vegan, gluten-free, lactose-free

 SERVES: 4

 PREP TIME: 10 MINUTES

 COOK TIME: 5 MINUTES

5 INGREDIENTS

- 2 slightly under ripe avocado, peeled, stone removed, thickly sliced
- 2 bunches of asparagus, woody ends trimmed off
- 1 15 oz (450 g) can of chickpeas, drained
- 1 small head of broccoli, broken into florets, stalk cut into matchsticks
- 4 cups (350g) of raw pea sprouts

From the pantry

- 1 tbsp ras el hanout
- 1 tsp olive oil
- 2 tbsp extra virgin olive oil
- 2 tsp apple cider vinegar
- Salt and pepper

METHOD:

1. Bring a pan of water to a boil and cook the broccoli florets and asparagus for about 4 minutes, until softened, but still with some crunch. Drain.
2. Meanwhile, heat a ridged griddle pan until very hot, and brush the avocado slices with the olive oil. Grill for just 30 seconds - 1 minute until you see char lines.
3. Toss the chickpeas with the ras el hanout and season to taste.
4. Mix the broccoli stalks, pea sprouts, extra virgin olive oil and vinegar together, and split between 2 shallow serving bowls.
5. Top with the broccoli florets, asparagus, chickpeas, and grilled avocado. Enjoy!
6. TIP: Some fresh herbs are good with this Buddha bowl as well. Try basil, parsley, or tarragon!

Nutritional Values, estimated per serving: Macros: Protein 10% / Fat 56% / Carbs 35%; Calories: 384 | Total carbs: 36 g | Net carbs: 19 g | Sugar: 7 g | Protein: 12 g | Fat: 25 g | Saturated fat: 3 g | Cholesterol: 0 mg | Sodium: 495 mg; Glycemic Load: 6.45

CHAPTER 5
SEAFOOD

TERIYAKI SALMON

pescetarian, lactose-free

 SERVES: 2

 PREP TIME: 5 MINUTES

 COOK TIME: 10 MINUTES

Marinade time:
30 minutes

5 INGREDIENTS

- 12 oz (330 g) salmon filet, skin removed, cut into chunks
- 2 tbsp white sesame seeds
- 4 baby bok choy, halved vertically
- 2 mild red chilis, sliced
- 2 tbsp teriyaki sauce

From the pantry
- 2 tbsp vegetable oil
- 1 tsp soy sauce

METHOD:

1. Toss the salmon chunks together with the teriyaki sauce and sesame seeds, and leave to marinate for 30 minutes.
2. Heat 1 tbsp of the oil in a large skillet or wok, over medium heat. Fry the chilis for 2 minutes, then add the bok choy.
3. Fry for another minute, then drizzle in the soy sauce, cover, and cook for about 3-4 minutes, until the bok choy has wilted. Remove from the pan and set aside.
4. Add the other tbsp of oil to the wok and turn up the heat. Add the salmon and fry for about 4-5 minutes, turning carefully, until just cooked through.
5. Return the bok choy to the pan and toss together gently. Divide between 2 plates, and enjoy!
6. TIP: Add some fresh aromatics to the dish! Chopped scallions, lemongrass, cilantro, or garlic chives are all good additions!

Nutritional Values, estimated per serving: Macros: Protein 38% / Fat 52% / Carbs 10%; Calories: 449 | Total carbs: 12 g | Net carbs: 8 g | Sugar: 7 g | Protein: 42 g | Fat: 27 g | Saturated fat: 4 g | Cholesterol: 78 mg | Sodium: 673 mg G; Glycemic Load: 3.58

SARDINE BRUSCHETTA

pescetarian

 SERVES: 2

 PREP TIME: 5 MINUTES

 COOK TIME: 0 MINUTES

5 INGREDIENTS

- 4 oz (110 g) can of sardines or herring in olive oil
- 6 small slices whole grain low-carb bread, toasted
- ¾ cup (180 g) ricotta cheese
- 2 tomatoes, sliced
- A few sprigs of parsley, roughly chopped

From the pantry
- Salt and pepper

METHOD:

1. Drain the sardines, reserving the oil.
2. Season the ricotta with plenty of black pepper, and a little salt if necessary.
3. Spread the ricotta on the toast, and top with the sliced tomatoes and the sardines.
4. Scatter with parsley, drizzle with a little of the reserved oil, and enjoy!
5. TIP: Flavor the ricotta if you like, for a little extra zing! Adding lemon and garlic really makes this dish sing!

Nutritional Values, estimated per serving: Macros: Protein 31% / Fat 42% / Carbs 27%; Calories: 440 | Total carbs: 30 g | Net carbs: 25 g | Sugar: 7 g | Protein: 32 g | Fat: 21 g | Saturated fat: 9 g | Cholesterol: 128 mg | Sodium: 457 mg; Glycemic Load: 11.60

STEAMED MUSSELS

pescetarian, gluten-free

 SERVES: 4

 PREP TIME: 20 MINUTES

 COOK TIME: 10 MINUTES

5 INGREDIENTS

- 4 lb (1.8 kg) live mussels
- 2 carrots, cut into batons
- 6 cloves of garlic, peeled and sliced
- 2 lemons, one zested and juiced, the other cut into quarters
- 1 small bunch of parsley, roughly chopped

From the pantry
- 2 tbsp olive oil

METHOD:

1. Clean the mussels, scrubbing them well, tugging off the hairy beards, and discarding any that are open and don't close when you tap them sharply.
2. Heat the olive oil over medium heat, in a pot large enough to contain all the mussels.
3. Add the carrots and sauté for about 5 minutes until softened, then add the garlic and lemon zest and fry for another 2 minutes.
4. Add the mussels and lemon juice, turn up the heat and cover the pot. Cook for about 5 minutes, shaking the pan occasionally, until the mussels have all opened. Season with black pepper, but you probably won't need any salt.
5. Discard any mussels that remain closed, scatter with the parsley and serve with the quartered lemons. Enjoy!
6. TIP: Serve with low-carb bread to mop up the juices, or just with a plain green salad for an ultra low-carb version!

Nutritional Values, estimated per serving: Macros: Protein 49% / Fat 32% / Carbs 19%; Calories: 480 | Total carbs: 24 g | Net carbs: 22 g | Sugar: 2 g | Protein: 55 g | Fat: 17 g | Saturated fat: 3 g | Cholesterol: 127 mg | Sodium: 1328 mg; Glycemic Load: 5.49

FISHCAKES

pescetarian, gluten-free, lactose-free

 SERVES: 2

 PREP TIME: 10 MINUTES

 COOK TIME: 6 MINUTES

5 INGREDIENTS

- 10 oz (280 g) fresh salmon filet, skin removed
- ¼ cup (30g) almond flour
- 1 egg
- 1 lemon, zest and juice
- 1 small bunch of chives, finely chopped

From the pantry
- 1 tbsp olive oil
- Salt and pepper

METHOD:

1. Mince the salmon very finely with the egg, lemon zest, and chives. (It's easiest to do this in the food processor.)
2. Add the almond flour to the mixture, season to taste, and press together into 6 little patties.
3. Heat the oil in a skillet over medium-high heat and fry for about 2-3 minutes on each side until golden brown and cooked through.
4. Serve hot, with lemon wedges to squeeze over, and enjoy!
5. TIP: Turn these into Thai-style fishcakes, by using lime instead of lemon, and adding scallions, chili, cilantro, lemongrass, and a dash of soy sauce to the mix!

Nutritional Values, estimated per serving: Macros: Protein 41% / Fat 55% / Carbs 4%; Calories: 367 | Total carbs: 4 g | Net carbs: 2 g | Sugar: 1 g | Protein: 36 g | Fat: 23 g | Saturated fat: 4 g | Cholesterol: 157 mg | Sodium: 481 mg; Glycemic Load: 2.53

GRILLED MACKEREL

pescetarian, gluten-free, lactose-free

SERVES: 2

PREP TIME: 10 MINUTES

COOK TIME: 10 MINUTES

5 INGREDIENTS

- 4 small mackerel filets, skin left on
- 2 red chilis, sliced
- ½ cup (50 g) green olives, pitted
- 1 cup (150 g) cherry tomatoes, halved
- 1 red onion, peeled and sliced

From the pantry

- 2 tbsp olive oil
- 1 tsp Italian seasoning
- 1 tbsp apple cider vinegar
- Salt and pepper

METHOD:

1. Heat 1 tbsp of the olive oil in a large skillet over medium heat and add the onions, Italian seasoning, and chilis, with a pinch of salt. Cook for about 5 minutes, until softened, but not colored.
2. Add the cherry tomatoes and olives and cook for another 2 minutes, then push the vegetables to the side of the pan. Add the other tbsp of oil and the mackerel filets, skin side down, and season.
3. Fry for about 3 minutes, then carefully flip, and drizzle over the vinegar.
4. Fry for another 3 minutes on the reverse side, then remove to the serving plates. Gently spoon over the vegetable mix and enjoy!
5. TIP: For extra crispy skin, dust the mackerel filets in 1 tsp of all-purpose flour before frying!

Nutritional Values, estimated per serving: Macros: Protein 27% / Fat 65% / Carbs 8%; Calories: 674 | Total carbs: 14 g | Net carbs: 10 g | Sugar: 7 g | Protein: 44 g | Fat: 49 g | Saturated fat: 10 g | Cholesterol: 157 mg | Sodium: 996 mg; Glycemic Load: 5.41

TUNA LETTUCE WRAP

pescetarian, gluten-free, lactose-free

SERVES: 2

PREP TIME: 5 MINUTES

COOK TIME: 0 MINUTES

5 INGREDIENTS

- 2 baby romaine lettuce, 8 outer leaves only
- 10 oz (280 g) canned tuna, drained
- ¼ cup (40 g) cooked corn
- 2 tbsp mayonnaise
- 6 radishes, diced

From the pantry

- Salt and pepper

METHOD:

1. Mix the tuna with the radishes, corn and mayonnaise, and season to taste.
2. Fill the lettuce leaves with the mix.
3. Eat by picking up with your hand, the lettuce encoding the filling. Enjoy!
4. TIP: Vary by adding different types of herbs to the mixture, or a squeeze of lemon or lime!

Nutritional Values, estimated per serving: Macros: Protein 48% / Fat 19% / Carbs 33%; Calories: 244 | Total carbs: 20 g | Net carbs: 17 g | Sugar: 2 g | Protein: 30 g | Fat: 5 g | Saturated fat: 1 g | Cholesterol: 54 mg | Sodium: 678 mg; Glycemic Load: 9.02

TiLAPiA WiTH CAULiFLOWER RiCE

pescetarian, gluten-free, lactose-free

 SERVES: 4

 PREP TIME: 10 MINUTES

 COOK TIME: 10 MINUTES

5 INGREDIENTS

- 4 tilapia filets (about 6-7 oz or 160-180 g each)
- 1 medium cauliflower
- 1 medium broccoli, broken into florets
- 1 small bunch of parsley, finely chopped
- 2 lemons, zest and juice of one, the other quartered

From the pantry
- 1 tbsp olive oil
- 1 tbsp extra virgin olive oil
- 1 tsp Italian seasoning
- Salt and pepper

METHOD:

1. Preheat the oven to 400°F.
2. Mix the olive oil with the Italian seasoning, lemon zest and juice, and a pinch of salt and pepper.
3. Put the broccoli florets into a baking dish, and lay the tilapia filets on top. Drizzle all over with the olive oil seasoning.
4. Bake for about 10 minutes, until the fish is cooked through and the broccoli has softened.
5. Meanwhile, grate the cauliflower with the coarsest edge of the grater, and mix with the extra virgin olive oil and most of the parsley. Season to taste.
6. Split the cauliflower between 4 serving plates and top with the roasted broccoli and tilapia filets. Garnish with the remaining parsley, and serve with lemon wedges on the side. Enjoy!
7. TIP: You can get spicer with the cauliflower rice if you want! Try toasting 1 tbsp each of coriander seed, fennel seed, and cumin seed, and mixing it in with the rice

Nutritional Values, estimated per serving: Macros: Protein 49% / Fat 28% / Carbs 23%; Calories: 361 | Total carbs: 24 g | Net carbs: 15 g | Sugar: 7 g | Protein: 47 g | Fat: 11 g | Saturated fat: 2 g | Cholesterol: 96 mg | Sodium: 855 mg; Glycemic Load: 2.48

FISH SKEWERS

pescetarian, gluten-free

 SERVES: 4

 PREP TIME: 10 MINUTES

 COOK TIME: 8 MINUTES

5 INGREDIENTS

- 1 ½ lb (675 g) firm white fish filets, e,g, cod, monkfish, hake, skin removed, cut into chunks
- 2 bell peppers, 1 yellow, 1 green, cut into chunks
- 1 red onion, cut into chunks
- 1 lemon, zest and juice
- 1 portion tzatziki

From the pantry
- 1 tbsp olive oil
- Salt and pepper

METHOD:

1. Mix the fish, bell peppers, onion, lemon juice and zest, and the olive oil together in a large bowl. Season with salt and pepper.
2. Thread tightly onto skewers, alternating the fish with different colored vegetables.
3. Grill over high heat for about 8 minutes, turning occasionally, until the vegetables are charred, and the fish is cooked through.
4. Serve hot, with tzatziki sauce on the side. Enjoy!
5. TIP: Try mixing up the vegetables! Zucchini, carrots, and fennel are all good here.

Nutritional Values, estimated per serving: Macros: Protein 61% / Fat 18% / Carbs 21%; Calories: 236 | Total carbs: 14 g | Net carbs: 12 g | Sugar: 5 g | Protein: 35 g | Fat: 5 g | Saturated fat: 1 g | Cholesterol: 83 mg | Sodium: 1126 mg; Glycemic Load: 5.03

ASIAN STEAMED FISH

pescetarian, lactose-free

 SERVES: 4

 PREP TIME: 10 MINUTES

 COOK TIME: 5 MINUTES

5 INGREDIENTS

- 4 white fish filets (e,g, cod, haddock, hake), about 7 oz (180 g) each
- 1 carrot, finely shredded
- 3 scallions, finely shredded
- 4 tbsp teriyaki sauce
- 1 small bunch of cilantro, leaves only

From the pantry
- 1 tbsp soy sauce
- Salt and pepper

METHOD:

1. Put the fish filets into a steamer basket, and season. Bring a pan of water to a boil and steam the fish over it, for about 5 minutes until just cooked through.
2. Mix the teriyaki sauce and soy sauce together.
3. Put the fish filets onto the serving plates, and drizzle over the sauce.
4. Top with the shredded vegetables and cilantro leaves. Enjoy!
5. TIP: Use some more vegetables to make the topping extra-colorful! Red or yellow bell peppers, radishes, or red cabbage all look very pretty!

Nutritional Values, estimated per serving: Macros: Protein 70% / Fat 20% / Carbs 10%; Calories: 211 | Total carbs: 5 g | Net carbs: 4 g | Sugar: 4 g | Protein: 35 g | Fat: 5 g | Saturated fat: 1 g | Cholesterol: 81 mg | Sodium: 685 mg; Glycemic Load: 2.78

ROASTED SALMON STEAK

pescetarian, gluten-free, lactose-free

 SERVES: 4

 PREP TIME: 10 MINUTES

 COOK TIME: 15 MINUTES

5 INGREDIENTS

- 2 lb (910 g) salmon, skin left on, cut into 4 large steaks
- 16 asparagus spears, woody ends removed
- 1 cup (150 g) of cherry tomatoes
- 2 lemon, 1 sliced, 1 quartered
- 1 head of garlic, sliced horizontally

From the pantry
- 3 tbsp olive oil
- Salt and pepper

METHOD:

1. Preheat the oven to 400°F.
2. Toss the asparagus, garlic, and cherry tomatoes with half of the olive oil and season. Put them in a baking dish.
3. Brush the salmon filets with the rest of the olive oil, and lie them on top of the vegetables. Season lightly, and divide the lemon slices between them.
4. Put the whole dish in the oven, and roast for about 15 minutes, until the salmon is cooked through.
5. Put one salmon steak on each plate, and divide the vegetables between them.
6. Squeeze out a little of the roasted garlic on the side, and serve with lemon quarters. Enjoy!
7. TIP: Add some fresh chopped herbs at the end, if you like! Parsley, dill, and tarragon are all good additions!

Nutritional Values, estimated per serving: Macros: Protein 49% / Fat 44% / Carbs 7%; Calories: 410 | Total carbs: 8 g | Net carbs: 7 g | Sugar: 2 g | Protein: 48 g | Fat: 20 g | Saturated fat: 3 g | Cholesterol: 104 mg | Sodium: 465 mg; Glycemic Load: 6.14

COD STEW WITH TOMATOES

pescetarian, gluten-free, lactose-free

 SERVES: 4

 PREP TIME: 10 MINUTES

 COOK TIME: 15 MINUTES

5 INGREDIENTS

- 1 ½ lb (675 g) cod filet, skin removed, cut into large chunks
- 1 15 oz (450 g) can of tomatoes
- 1 15 oz (450 g) can of chickpeas
- 1 cup (100 g) of green olives, pitted
- 1 onion, peeled and sliced

From the pantry

- 2 tbsp olive oil
- 1 tbsp ras el hanout
- 1 tsp harissa chili paste
- Salt and pepper

METHOD:

1. Warm the olive oil in a large pan over medium heat. Add the onion with a pinch of salt and fry until softened and starting to color at the edges, about 8-10 minutes.
2. Add the harissa, ras el hanout, olives and chickpeas, along with the liquid in the can. Keep cooking for a couple of minutes, then add the tomatoes.
3. Bring to a boil, simmer for a few minutes, then add the cod. Cover, and keep cooking at a low temperature for about 5 minutes, until the fish is cooked through. Season to taste.
4. Serve with whole grain, low carb bread, and enjoy!
5. TIP: Boost vitamins and minerals by adding leafy greens! Wilt a handful of spinach leaves, chard, or spring greens in the stew for the last few minutes of cooking.

Nutritional Values, estimated per serving: Macros: Protein 39% / Fat 35% / Carbs 26%; Calories: 342 | Total carbs: 23 g | Net carbs: 14 g | Sugar: 4 g | Protein: 33 g | Fat: 14 g | Saturated fat: 2 g | Cholesterol: 80 mg | Sodium: 1344 mg; Glycemic Load: 7.35

GARLIC SHRIMP KONJAC NOODLES

pescetarian, gluten-free, lactose-free

 SERVES: 2

 PREP TIME: 5 MINUTES

 COOK TIME: 10 MINUTES

5 INGREDIENTS

- 8 oz (225 g) raw shrimp, peeled
- 8 oz (225 g) of konjac noodles
- 6 cloves garlic, peeled and minced
- 1 small bunch of parsley, finely chopped
- 1 lemon, zest and juice

From the pantry

- 2 tbsp olive oil
- Salt and pepper

METHOD:

1. Warm the olive oil in a pan over medium-low heat, and add the garlic. Fry for 2 minutes, then add the shrimp and the lemon zest.
2. Turn up the heat and cook for 2-3 minutes until the shrimp are just cooked through. Mix in the lemon juice and parsley, and season to taste.
3. Meanwhile, cook the konjac noodles according to package instructions.
4. Toss the noodles with the shrimp mix, and enjoy!
5. TIP: A pinch of red pepper flakes is a good addition if you like it spicy!

Nutritional Values, estimated per serving: Macros: Protein 39% / Fat 52% / Carbs 9%; Calories: 255 | Total carbs: 10 g | Net carbs: 6 g | Sugar: 1 g | Protein: 24 g | Fat: 14 g | Saturated fat: 2 g | Cholesterol: 183 mg | Sodium: 444 mg; Glycemic Load: 2.01

FRIED SOLE WITH VEGGIES

pescetarian, gluten-free, lactose-free

 SERVES: 2

 PREP TIME: 10 MINUTES

 COOK TIME: 25 MINUTES

5 INGREDIENTS

- 2 Dover (6 oz/160 g each) sole filets
- 2 bell peppers, red and yellow
- 1 zucchini, cut into batons
- ½ small broccoli, broken into florets
- 1 large onion, peeled and sliced

From the pantry

- 2 tbsp olive oil
- 1 tsp Italian seasoning
- Salt and pepper

METHOD:

1. Heat 1 tbsp of olive oil in a large skillet over medium heat. Add the onion with a pinch of salt, and sauté until golden brown and caramelized, about 15-20 minutes. Lift out of the pan with a slotted spoon and set aside.
2. Add the broccoli, zucchini and bell peppers, and cook for about 5 minutes, until colored in places, but still crunchy. Lift out and divide between the 2 serving plates.
3. Add the other tbsp of oil and turn the heat up to medium high. Fry the fish for about 2-3 minutes on each side, until golden brown, crusty and cooked through. Season to taste.
4. Lift the fish out carefully onto the serving plates, and add a spoon of caramelized onions. Enjoy!
5. TIP: If you don't have time for the caramelized onions, a spoonful of sauerkraut makes a good replacement.

Nutritional Values, estimated per serving: Macros: Protein 28% / Fat 32% / Carbs 41%; Calories: 383 | Total carbs: 32 g | Net carbs: 24 g | Sugar: 8 g | Protein: 28 g | Fat: 18 g | Saturated fat: 3 g | Cholesterol: 73 mg | Sodium: 703 mg; Glycemic Load: 8.82

SHRIMP SALAD WITH AVOCADO

pescetarian, gluten-free, lactose-free

 SERVES: 2

 PREP TIME: 5 MINUTES

 COOK TIME: 5 MINUTES

5 INGREDIENTS

- 8 oz (225 g) raw shrimp, peeled
- 2 medium tomatoes, chopped
- 1 medium avocado, peeled, stoned and chopped
- 2 limes, juice only
- 1 bunch of cilantro, roughly chopped

From the pantry

- 1 tbsp olive oil
- 2 tbsp extra virgin olive oil
- Salt and pepper
- ½ tsp harissa chili paste

METHOD:

1. Heat the olive oil in a skillet over medium heat, and fry the shrimp with a pinch of salt until just cooked through, about 2-3 minutes.
2. Mix the extra virgin olive oil with the lime juice and harissa paste, and season to taste.
3. Toss the cooked shrimp together with the tomatoes, avocado, cilantro, and dressing, and enjoy!
4. TIP: You can use the same technique with any diced white fish, or even salmon or tuna instead of shrimp. If you have really good sushi-grade seafood, you can even use it raw and let it marinade in the lime juice for ceviche.

Nutritional Values, estimated per serving: Macros: Protein 22% / Fat 66% / Carbs 13%; Calories: 472 | Total carbs: 18 g | Net carbs: 9 g | Sugar: 5 g | Protein: 26 g | Fat: 36 g | Saturated fat: 5 g | Cholesterol: 183 mg | Sodium: 462 mg; Glycemic Load: 4.66

PAN-FRIED SALMON WITH RED CABBAGE

pescetarian, gluten-free, lactose-free

 SERVES: 4

 PREP TIME: 10 MINUTES

 COOK TIME: 25 MINUTES

5 INGREDIENTS

- 2 lb (900 g) salmon filet, cut into 8 small steaks
- ½ small red cabbage, shredded
- 1 tbsp ginger, peeled and minced
- 1 cup chicken broth
- 1 small bunch of parsley

From the pantry
- 2 tbsp olive oil
- 1 tsp Italian seasoning
- 1 tbsp apple cider vinegar
- Salt and pepper

METHOD:

1. Mix 1 tbsp of olive oil with the ginger, Italian seasoning, and salt and pepper. Rub it all over the salmon steaks, and set aside to marinate.
2. Put the cabbage into a large pan, along with the vinegar and broth, and a pinch of salt. Set over a medium-low heat, bring to a boil, then turn down to a simmer. Cook for about 15 minutes, partly covered, until the cabbage is completely soft, and the liquid has almost all boiled away. Season to taste.
3. Heat the other tbsp of olive oil in a large skillet over medium-high heat. Add the salmon steaks, and fry for about 4 minutes on each side, until cooked through.
4. Put a spoonful of red cabbage on each plate, topped with 2 salmon steaks. Season to taste, garnish with the parsley and enjoy!
5. TIP: This works with white cabbage as well - or even chinese cabbage or bok choy for an Asian influence!

Nutritional Values, estimated per serving: Macros: Protein 51% / Fat 39% / Carbs 10%; Calories: 410 | Total carbs: 11 g | Net carbs: 8 g | Sugar: 5 g | Protein: 50 g | Fat: 18 g | Saturated fat: 3 g | Cholesterol: 106 mg | Sodium: 584 mg; Glycemic Load: 4.87

GRILLED HAKE

pescetarian, gluten-free, lactose-free

 SERVES: 4

 PREP TIME: 5 MINUTES

 COOK TIME: 15 MINUTES

5 INGREDIENTS

- 4 hake filets (about 8 oz/225 g each)
- 2 medium zucchini, cut into thick rounds
- 1 red bell pepper, cut into chunks
- 1 lemon, sliced
- 2 scallions, sliced, whites and green separated

From the pantry
- 2 tbsp olive oil
- 1 tsp ras el hanout
- Salt and pepper

METHOD:

1. Preheat the overhead grill. Mix the ras el hanout with 1 tbsp of oil, season, and rub it over the fish filets.
2. Put the zucchini, bell pepper and scallion whites into a roasting pan, toss with 1 tbsp of the olive oil and season well.
3. Grill the vegetables for about 10 minutes, until golden-brown and slightly charred in places.
4. Lay the hake filets on top of the vegetables and grill for another 5 minutes, until the fish is cooked.
5. Divide the vegetables between each plate and top with a piece of hake. Scatter with the scallion greens, and serve with the lemon slices. Enjoy!
6. TIP: Fresh basil is a lovely summery garnish for this recipe! You could also try crushing on some raw garlic at the end.

Nutritional Values, estimated per serving: Macros: Protein 67% / Fat 25% / Carbs 8%; Calories: 305 | Total carbs: 7 g | Net carbs: 5 g | Sugar: 4 g | Protein: 48 g | Fat: 9 g | Saturated fat: 1 g | Cholesterol: 154 mg | Sodium: 1243 mg; Glycemic Load: 2.44

FISH BURGER

pescetarian

 SERVES: 2

 PREP TIME: 5 MINUTES

 COOK TIME: 5 MINUTES

5 INGREDIENTS

- 2 small cod filets, about 6 oz (160 g) each, skin removed
- 2 low-carb bread rolls, toasted if you like
- ½ cup (10 g)of arugula
- 4 radishes, sliced
- 2 tbsp tzatziki sauce

From the pantry
- 1 tbsp olive oil
- ½ tsp garam masala
- Salt and pepper

METHOD:

1. Rub the garam masala all over the cod filets and season.
2. Heat the olive oil in a small skillet over medium-high heat. Fry the cod filets for about 4 minutes each side, until cooked through.
3. Meanwhile, split open the bread rolls, spread the tzatziki on the lower half, and add the arugula and radishes.
4. Carefully put the cod filets on top of the salad, close the bread roll, and enjoy!
5. TIP: This makes an Indian-flavored burger, but you could change the spice rub if you liked. Try Italian seasoning for a more European version!

Nutritional Values, estimated per serving: Macros: Protein 49% / Fat 26 % / Carbs 25 %; Calories: 285 | Total carbs: 18 g | Net carbs: 16 g | Sugar: 1 g | Protein: 33g | Fat: 8 g | Saturated fat: 1 g | Cholesterol: 81 mg | Sodium: 834 mg; Glycemic Load: 10.68

KERALAN FISH CURRY

pescetarian, gluten-free, lactose-free

 SERVES: 4

 PREP TIME: 10 MINUTES

 COOK TIME: 15 MINUTES

5 INGREDIENTS

- 2 lb (900 g) white fish filet (e.g. cod, hake, haddock, monkfish), cut into chunks
- 3 tbsp ginger, peeled and minced
- 6 cloves of garlic, peeled and sliced
- 2 onions, peeled and sliced
- 2 15 oz (450 g) can of tomatoes
- Optional: 1 bunch of cilantro, roughly chopped

From the pantry
- 1 tbsp vegetable oil
- 1 tbsp garam masala
- 1 tsp harissa chili paste
- Salt and pepper

METHOD:

1. Warm the oil in a large pan over medium heat. Add the onion with a pinch of salt and fry until softened and starting to color at the edges, about 8-10 minutes.
2. Add the harissa, garlic, ginger, and garam masala. Keep cooking for a couple of minutes, then add the tomatoes.
3. Bring to a boil, simmer for a few minutes, then add the fish. Cover, and keep cooking at a low temperature for about 5 minutes, until the fish is cooked through. Season to taste.
4. Optionally garnish with cilantro leaves, and enjoy!
5. TIP: Serve with low-carb Indian flatbread, or a small portion of whole grain rice.

Nutritional Values, estimated per serving: Macros: Protein 64% / Fat 19% / Carbs 17%; Calories: 240 | Total carbs: 11 g | Net carbs: 6 g | Sugar: 6 g | Protein: 37 g | Fat: 5 g | Saturated fat: 1 g | Cholesterol: 107 mg | Sodium: 1244 mg; Glycemic Load: 7.00

SARDINE STUFFED BELL PEPPERS

pescetarian, gluten-free, lactose-free

 SERVES: 2

 PREP TIME: 10 MINUTES

 COOK TIME: 20 MINUTES

5 INGREDIENTS

- 4 oz (110 g) can of sardines or herring in olive oil
- 2 small bell peppers, top removed, hollowed out
- ½ cup (100 g) cooked brown rice
- 1 small celeriac, peeled and cut into wedges
- 1 tsp grainy mustard

From the pantry
- 1 tsp harissa paste
- 1 tbsp olive oil
- Salt and pepper

METHOD:

1. Preheat the oven to 400ºC.
2. Toss the celeriac with the olive oil and harissa paste, and season.
3. Mix the sardines with the rice, mustard, and some of the oil from the can, and season to taste. Use the mix to stuff the bell peppers.
4. Put both the stuffed peppers and the celeriac wedges in a roasting pan, and roast for 20 minutes, until the vegetables are cooked.
5. Serve hot, with salad on the side, and enjoy!
6. TIP: Try chopped cucumbers and tomatoes as a tasty healthy side dish!

Nutritional Values, estimated per serving: Macros: Protein 22% / Fat 34% / Carbs 44%; Calories: 377 | Total carbs: 42 g | Net carbs: 34 g | Sugar: 9 g | Protein: 21 g | Fat: 15 g | Saturated fat: 2 g | Cholesterol: 81 mg | Sodium: 675 mg; Glycemic Load: 10.93

FISH CASSEROLE

pescetarian, gluten-free

 SERVES: 4

 PREP TIME: 5 MINUTES

 COOK TIME: 15 MINUTES

5 INGREDIENTS

- 2 lb (900 g) white fish filets, cut into chunks (e.g. cod, hake, haddock, monkfish)
- 1 cup of heavy cream (low fat, if you like)
- 1 bunch of dill, roughly chopped
- 1 tbsp black sesame seeds
- 6 cloves of garlic, peeled and crushed

From the pantry
- 1 tsp olive oil
- Salt and pepper

METHOD:

1. Preheat the oven to 325ºF.
2. Use the oil to grease a baking dish.
3. Mix the fish with the cream, dill and garlic, and season well. Tip it into the baking dish, and scatter with the sesame seeds.
4. Bake for about 15 minutes, until the fish is cooked through, and golden brown on top.
5. Serve hot, with a fresh green salad on the side. Enjoy!
6. TIP: Try mixing a tbsp of grainy mustard in with the cream, for a slightly Nordic flavor!

Nutritional Values, estimated per serving: Macros: Protein 52% / Fat 43% / Carbs 5%; Calories: 298 | Total carbs: 4 g | Net carbs: 4 g | Sugar: 2 g | Protein: 37 g | Fat: 15 g | Saturated fat: 7 g | Cholesterol: 136 mg | Sodium: 1008 mg; Glycemic Load: 2.60

CHAPTER 6
MEAT AND POULTRY

JAPANESE CHICKEN-GINGER MEATBALLS

lactose-free

 SERVES: 2

 PREP TIME: 15 MINUTES

 COOK TIME: 5 MINUTES

5 INGREDIENTS

- ½ lb (225 g) ground chicken
- 2 tbsp ginger, peeled and minced
- 2 tbsp sesame seeds
- 2 scallions, chopped, whites and green divided
- 1 tbsp teriyaki sauce

From the pantry
- 1 tbsp vegetable oil
- Salt and pepper

METHOD:

1. Mix the chicken with the ginger, scallion whites, half of the sesame seeds, and season.
2. Roll into 12 little meatballs.
3. Heat the oil in a skillet over medium heat, and fry the meatballs for about 3-4 minutes each side, until browned on the outside and cooked through.
4. Add the teriyaki sauce to the skillet and swirl, so the meatballs are coated in the sticky sauce.
5. Put onto a serving plate, scatter with the rest of the sesame seeds and the scallion greens, and enjoy!
6. TIP: If you want to turn this appetizer into an entrée, serve the meatballs with steamed Asian greens, and/or Konjac noodles!

<u>Nutritional Values, estimated per serving:</u> Macros: Protein 30% / Fat 64% / Carbs 6%; Calories: 290 | Total carbs: 5 g | Net carbs: 4 g | Sugar: 2 g | Protein: 22 g | Fat: 21 g | Saturated fat: 4 g | Cholesterol: 98 mg | Sodium: 526 mg; Glycemic Load: 2.96

LENTIL STEW WITH BACON

gluten-free, lactose-free

 SERVES: 4

 PREP TIME: 10 MINUTES

 COOK TIME: 20 MINUTES

5 INGREDIENTS

- 8 oz (225 g) bacon, diced
- 1 ½ cup (325 g) dried green or brown lentils
- 2 carrots, diced
- 4 ribs of celery
- 1 quart (950 ml) chicken stock

From the pantry
- 2 tbsp olive oil
- 1 tbsp tomato paste
- Salt and pepper

METHOD:

1. Heat the olive oil in a large pan over medium heat and add the onion with a pinch of salt. Fry for about 8-10 minutes, until starting to soften and color at the edges.
2. Add the carrots, bacon, and tomato paste. Continue frying for another 5 minutes until the fat has started to render from the bacon, and it's turning golden brown in places.
3. Add the lentils and the chicken stock and bring to a boil. Turn down to a simmer and cook until the lentils are tender, about 15 minutes.
4. Season to taste, and enjoy!
5. TIP: Mix in some other low-carb veggies if you like, or add an onion.

<u>Nutritional Values, estimated per serving:</u> Macros: Protein 16% / Fat 58% / Carbs 26%; Calories: 502| Total carbs: 32 g | Net carbs: 24 g | Sugar: 10 g | Protein: 21 g | Fat: 33 g | Saturated fat: 9 g | Cholesterol: 45 mg | Sodium: 1198 mg; Glycemic Load: 14.54

MOROCCAN BEEF TAGINE STEW

gluten-free, lactose-free

 SERVES: 4

 PREP TIME: 10 MINUTES

 COOK TIME: 1 HOUR 30 MINUTES

5 INGREDIENTS

- 2 lb (900 g) stewing beef, cut into chunks
- 1 15 oz (450 g) can tomatoes
- 2 onions, peeled and sliced
- ½ cup (20 g) dried apricots or prunes (or a mixture), cut in half
- 2 tbsp slivered almonds

From the pantry

- 2 tbsp ras el hanout
- 1 tbsp tomato paste
- 2 tbsp olive oil
- Salt and pepper

METHOD:

1. Heat half the olive oil in a large pan over medium-high heat and add the beef. Sear on all sides until golden brown, then lift out with a slotted spoon and set aside.
2. Put the rest of the oil in the same pan, then add the onion with a pinch of salt. Fry for about 8-10 minutes, until starting to soften and color at the edges.
3. Return the meat to the pan and add the ras el hanout and tomato paste. Continue frying for another few minutes, then add the apricots or prunes, and the tomatoes. Top up with just enough water to cover the meat.
4. Bring to a boil, then turn down to a simmer and cook until the beef is very tender, about an hour or a little longer.
5. Season to taste, scatter over the almonds, and enjoy!
6. TIP: Freshly chopped parsley or mint makes a lovely fresh garnish for this stew!

Nutritional Values, estimated per serving: Macros: Protein 44% / Fat 39% / Carbs 17%; Calories: 480 | Total carbs: 23 g | Net carbs: 17 g | Sugar: 15 g | Protein: 53 g | Fat: 21 g | Saturated fat: 6 g | Cholesterol: 145 mg | Sodium: 603 mg; Glycemic Load: 8.72

STIR FRIED CHICKEN NOODLES

lactose-free

 SERVES: 4

 PREP TIME: 5 MINUTES

 COOK TIME: 10 MINUTES

5 INGREDIENTS

- 4 chicken breasts (6oz/170 g each), skin removed, cut into chunks
- 1 lb (450 g) Konjac noodles
- 4 cloves garlic, peeled and sliced
- 2 tbsp ginger, peeled and minced
- 1 lb (450 g) mixed vegetables for stir fry - carrots, mushrooms, bell peppers, zucchini, etc

From the pantry

- 2 tbsp soy sauce
- 1 tsp harissa paste
- 1 tbsp vegetable oil
- Salt and pepper

METHOD:

1. Heat the oil in a wok over medium heat and add the chicken with a pinch of salt. Fry briskly until browned on the outside, about 4 minutes.
2. Add the vegetables, garlic, ginger, and harissa paste. Carry on cooking for another 3-4 minutes, until the chicken is cooked through and the vegetables have browned in places.
3. Meanwhile, cook the konjac noodles according to packet instructions.
4. Add the cooked noodles to the wok, along with the soy sauce. Toss together, season to taste, and enjoy!
5. TIP: Try garnishing with fresh cilantro and/or some toasted sesame seeds

Nutritional Values, estimated per serving: Macros: Protein 67% / Fat 15% / Carbs 17%; Calories: 554 | Total carbs: 27 g | Net carbs: 19 g | Sugar: 4 g | Protein: 62 g | Fat: 10 g | Saturated fat: 2 g | Cholesterol: 188 mg | Sodium: 330 mg; Glycemic Load: 4.56

MEXICAN CHILI BEAN SOUP

gluten-free, lactose-free

 SERVES: 4

 PREP TIME: 10 MINUTES

 COOK TIME: 15 MINUTES

5 INGREDIENTS

- 1 15 oz (450 g) can of kidney beans
- 1 15 oz (450 g) can of chili tomatoes
- 1 lb (450 g) ground beef
- 4 ribs of celery, chopped
- 2 large onions, peeled and chopped

From the pantry
- 1 tbsp olive oil
- 2 tbsp tomato paste
- 1 tsp harissa chili paste
- 1 tsp garam masala
- 1 tsp ras el hanout

METHOD:

1. Heat the olive oil in a large pan over medium heat, and add the onions with a pinch of salt. Fry until softened and starting to color in places, about 8-10 minutes.
2. Add the celery and the ground beef and carry on cooking for another 5 minutes, breaking up the meat with a spoon, until the beef has lost its raw pink look.
3. Add the chili paste, tomato paste and the spices and stir in.
4. Add the tomatoes, the kidney beans plus the liquid from the can, and bring to a boil. Turn the heat down to a simmer, and cook for about 20 minutes, until the meat is cooked through and the sauce has thickened slightly.
5. Serve hot, with sour cream and fresh cilantro if you like, and enjoy!
6. TIP: Sour cream is a great addition to this Mexican inspired dish, to cut through that chili heat. Put a pot on the table, so people can help themselves!

Nutritional Values, estimated per serving: Macros: Protein 17% / Fat 62% / Carbs 21%; Calories: 558 | Total carbs: 30 g | Net carbs: 20 g | Sugar: 9 g | Protein: 24 g | Fat: 38 g | Saturated fat: 14 g | Cholesterol: 88 mg | Sodium: 529 mg; Glycemic Load: 10.17

ROASTED BRUSSELS SPROUTS WITH BACON

gluten-free, lactose-free

 SERVES: 4 AS A SIDE

 PREP TIME: 10 MINUTES

 COOK TIME: 30 MINUTES

5 INGREDIENTS

- 1 lb (450 g)Brussels sprouts, trimmed and halved
- 8 oz (225 g) pancetta or bacon, diced
- 1 sprig of thyme
- ½ cup (50 g) Parmesan cheese, grated
- 1 lemon, zest and juice

From the pantry
- 2 tbsp olive oil
- Salt and pepper

METHOD

1. Preheat the oven to 420°F.
2. Toss the Brussels sprouts with the olive oil, bacon, and thyme, and season with salt and pepper.
3. Roast in the hot oven for about 25 minutes, until golden brown at the edges.
4. Scatter over the Parmesan and lemon zest and squeeze over the lemon juice. Return to the oven for just another 3-4 minutes.
5. Serve with your favorite steak or chicken filet, and enjoy!
6. TIP: If you like it spicy, try adding a pinch of red pepper flakes along with the parmesan and lemon zest!

Nutritional Values, estimated per serving: Macros: Protein 14% / Fat 74% / Carbs 12%; Calories: 400 | Total carbs: 13 g | Net carbs: 9 g | Sugar: 3 g | Protein: 15 g | Fat: 33 g | Saturated fat: 10 g | Cholesterol: 48 mg | Sodium: 775 mg; Glycemic Load: 2.47

LENTILS WITH GRILLED CHICKEN BREAST

gluten-free, lactose-free

 SERVES: 2

 PREP TIME: 5 MINUTES

 COOK TIME: 25 MINUTES

5 INGREDIENTS

- 10 oz (280 g) chicken tenders
- ¾ cup (130 g) dry brown lentils
- ½ cup (75 g) cherry tomatoes, halved
- 1 onion, peeled and diced
- 1 bunch of parsley, roughly chopped

From the pantry

- 2 tbsp olive oil
- 1 tbsp extra virgin olive oil
- 1 tsp Italian seasoning
- 1 tsp apple cider vinegar
- Salt and pepper

METHOD:

1. In a large pan, heat 1 tbsp olive oil over medium heat and add the onion with a pinch of salt, and the Italian seasoning. Fry for about 8-10 minutes, until softened and starting to color at the edges.
2. Add the lentils, and stir to combine. Pour in enough water to cover the lentils by about ½ inch, and bring to a boil. Turn down the heat and simmer for about 12-15 minutes, until the lentils are cooked through. Top up with more water if you need to.
3. Meanwhile, heat the other tbsp of olive oil in a skillet over medium-high heat. Add the chicken tenders. Fry for about 3-4 minutes, until golden and crispy, then turn and fry on the reverse side for about another 3 minutes, until cooked through. Leave to rest.
4. Add the tomatoes to the lentil mix and let them soften a little in the heat. Stir in the parsley, extra virgin olive oil, and vinegar, and season to taste.
5. Put a spoon of cooked lentils on the serving plates, and scatter the chicken tenders over. Use a little extra fresh parsley to garnish. Enjoy!
6. TIP: You can add in some extra veggies to the lentils, if you like! Diced celery, or zucchini, or mushrooms are all great!

Nutritional Values, estimated per serving: Macros: Protein 35% / Fat 45% / Carbs 20%; Calories: 461 | Total carbs: 24 g | Net carbs: 15 g | Sugar: 5 g | Protein: 40 g | Fat: 23 g | Saturated fat: 11 g | Cholesterol: 81 mg | Sodium: 386 mg; Glycemic Load: 15.75

TURKEY PATTIES WITH SALAD

gluten-free, lactose-free

 SERVES: 2

 PREP TIME: 10 MINUTES

 COOK TIME: 10 MINUTES

5 INGREDIENTS

- 12 oz (330 g) ground turkey
- 1 egg
- 2 cups (60 g) of salad greens
- 1 cup (150 g) of cherry tomatoes, quartered
- 1 small cucumber, sliced, or cut into ribbons

From the pantry

- 1 tbsp olive oil
- 1 tbsp extra virgin olive oil
- 1 tsp apple cider vinegar
- Salt and pepper

METHOD:

1. Mix the turkey with the egg and season generously. Shape into 8 small patties.
2. Heat the olive oil in a skillet over medium-high heat, and fry the turkey patties for about 4-5 minutes each side, until golden brown and cooked through.
3. Meanwhile, mix the extra virgin olive oil and vinegar together to make a salad dressing, and season.
4. Toss the salad greens, cucumber and tomatoes together with the dressing.
5. Divide the salad between 2 serving plates, and put 4 turkey patties on each one. Enjoy!
6. TIP: Vary up the flavor by trying out different spices in the turkey patties! Go spicy with a chili paste, Arabic with some sumac and lemon zest, or Spanish with smoked paprika and cumin!

Nutritional Values, estimated per serving: Macros: Protein 35% / Fat 59% / Carbs 6%; Calories: 445 | Total carbs: 7 g | Net carbs: 4 g | Sugar: 4 g | Protein: 39 g | Fat: 29 g | Saturated fat: 6 g | Cholesterol: 210 mg | Sodium: 442 mg; Glycemic Load: 5.10

THAI BAKED CHICKEN

gluten-free, lactose-free

 SERVES: 4

 PREP TIME: 5 MINUTES

 COOK TIME: 25 MINUTES

5 INGREDIENTS

- 4 chicken thighs, boned
- 2 cups (320 g) of peas
- 1 tbsp Thai red curry paste
- 2 limes, zest and juice of 1, the other sliced
- 6 cloves of garlic, peeled and crushed

From the pantry
- 1 tbsp vegetable oil
- 2 tbsp soy sauce
- Salt and pepper

METHOD:

1. Mix the vegetable oil, soy sauce, curry paste, garlic, lime juice and lime zest together. Put the chicken in a roasting pan, and rub the curry mix all over it. Set aside to marinate for 30 minutes.
2. Preheat the oven to 425°F.
3. Bake the chicken in the hot oven for 15 minutes, then add the peas, tossing to coat them in the hot spicy fat.
4. Return to the oven and bake for another 5-10 minutes, until the chicken is cooked through and golden brown.
5. Season to taste, and serve with lime sliced on the side. Enjoy!
6. TIP: Try serving with a cucumber salad, and plenty of fresh Thai basil and mint!

Nutritional Values, estimated per serving: Macros: Protein 29% / Fat 66% / Carbs 5%; Calories: 492 | Total carbs: 7 g | Net carbs: 5 g | Sugar: 2 g | Protein: 34 g | Fat: 36 g | Saturated fat: 9 g | Cholesterol: 189 mg | Sodium: 560 mg; Glycemic Load: 6.32

CHICKEN CACCIATORE

gluten-free, lactose-free

 SERVES: 4

 PREP TIME: 5 MINUTES

 COOK TIME: 25 MINUTES

5 INGREDIENTS

- 8 chicken drumsticks
- 2 red bell peppers, cut into chunks.
- ½ cup (50 g) black olives, pitted
- 1 15 oz (450 g) jar of low-sugar marinara sauce
- 2 large onions, peeled and sliced

From the pantry
- 2 tbsp olive oil
- 1 tsp Italian seasoning
- Salt and pepper

METHOD:

1. Preheat the oven to 400°F.
2. Mix all the ingredients together in a large baking dish. Bake for about 25 minutes, until the chicken is golden brown and cooked through. Season to taste.
3. Serve with fresh herbs, if you like, and enjoy!
4. TIP: Fresh herb leaves spike up the flavor even more. Try tucking in some bay leaves for a more wintery vibe, or scatter over fresh basil at the end to evoke summer.

Nutritional Values, estimated per serving: Macros: Protein 24% / Fat 63% / Carbs 13%; Calories: 605 | Total carbs: 20 g | Net carbs: 15 g | Sugar: 12 g | Protein: 35 g | Fat: 42 g | Saturated fat: 10 g | Cholesterol: 191 mg | Sodium: 1022 mg; Glycemic Load: 8.31

CHICKEN KEBAB

gluten-free, lactose-free

 SERVES: 2

 PREP TIME: 10 MINUTES

 COOK TIME: 10 MINUTES

5 INGREDIENTS

- 2 medium size chicken breasts, skin removed, cut into chunks (~ 6oz/170 g each)
- 1 onion, peeled and cut into chunks
- 2 bell peppers, 1 red, 1 yellow, cut into chunks
- 1 tbsp grainy mustard
- 1 lemon

From the pantry
- 1 tbsp olive oil
- Salt and pepper

METHOD:

1. Zest and juice half the lemon, and mix with the olive oil and mustard, and season generously.
2. Toss the chicken, onion, and bell peppers in the olive oil mix, and thread onto skewers, alternating meat with vegetables.
3. Under a hot grill, or on a griddle pan, grill the kebabs for about 10 minutes, turning frequently, until the chicken is cooked through.
4. Cut the other half lemon into wedges, and squeeze over the juice at the table. Enjoy!
5. TIP: Serve with a low-carb dip on the side, like a low-sugar ketchup, or tzatziki.

Nutritional Values, estimated per serving: Macros: Protein 55% / Fat 27% / Carbs 19%; Calories: 360 | Total carbs: 19 g | Net carbs: 16 g | Sugar: 3 g | Protein: 55 g | Fat: 11 g | Saturated fat: 2 g | Cholesterol: 114 mg | Sodium: 776 mg; Glycemic Load: 7.25

PORK CHOP WITH GREMOLATA

gluten-free, lactose-free

 SERVES: 2

 PREP TIME: 5 MINUTES

 COOK TIME: 12 MINUTES

5 INGREDIENTS

- 2 pork chops (~ 6 oz/170 g each)
- 1 portion gremolata
- 1 tbsp mustard
- 1 lemon, halved
- 2 tbsp parmesan, grated

From the pantry
- 1 tbsp olive oil
- Salt and pepper

METHOD:

1. Mix the olive oil with the mustard and season generously. Brush it all over the pork chops.
2. Heat a skillet over medium high heat, and add the pork chops. Fry for about 5-6 minutes each side, until cooked through.
3. For the last few minutes of cooking, add the lemon halves to the pan, cut side down.
4. Put the pork chops on the serving plates, and scatter over the parmesan. Top with generous spoonfuls of gremolata and enjoy!
5. TIP: Serve with the green beans on page 35, as a side dish!

Nutritional Values, estimated per serving: Macros: Protein 42% / Fat 53% / Carbs 6%; Calories: 444 | Total carbs: 8 g | Net carbs: 6 g | Sugar: 2 g | Protein: 44 g | Fat: 26 g | Saturated fat: 7 g | Cholesterol: 135 mg | Sodium: 566 mg; Glycemic Load: 7.25

CHORIZO WITH CHICKPEAS

gluten-free, lactose-free

 SERVES: 4

 PREP TIME: 10 MINUTES

 COOK TIME: 15 MINUTES

5 INGREDIENTS

- 12 oz (330 g) spicy chorizo sausage, cut into chunks
- 1 red bell pepper, cut into chunks
- 1 15 oz (450 g) jar of low-sugar marinara sauce
- 1 15 oz (450 g) can of chickpeas
- 1 tbsp of smoked paprika

From the pantry
- 1 tbsp olive oil
- Salt and pepper

METHOD:

1. Warm the olive oil in a large pan over medium heat and add the chorizo. Fry for about 2-3 minutes until the fat starts to render and the oil is bright red.
2. Add the bell pepper, and smoked paprika and fry for 2 minutes more.
3. Add the marinara sauce, chickpeas, and the liquid in the can. Bring to a boil, then turn down to a simmer. Cook for about 10 minutes, until the sauce thickens slightly.
4. Can be served immediately, hot, or left to cool to room temperature. Enjoy!
5. TIP: Add in some chicken as well, for a high-protein version!

Nutritional Values, estimated per serving: Macros: Protein 20% / Fat 62% / Carbs 18%; Calories: 579 | Total carbs: 27 g | Net carbs: 19 g | Sugar: 7 g | Protein: 28 g | Fat: 40 g | Saturated fat: 13 g | Cholesterol: 77 mg | Sodium: 1526 mg; Glycemic Load: 7.54

MEATBALLS IN TOMATO SAUCE

gluten-free, lactose-free

 SERVES: 4

 PREP TIME: 10 MINUTES

 COOK TIME: 25 MINUTES

5 INGREDIENTS

- 1 lb (450 g) ground pork
- 1 egg
- 1 cup (60 g) whole grain fresh breadcrumbs
- 2 onions, peeled and sliced
- 1 15 oz (450 g) jar of low-sugar marinara sauce

From the pantry
- 1 tbsp olive oil
- 1 tsp Italian seasoning
- Salt and pepper

METHOD:

1. Mix the ground pork with the egg, breadcrumbs, Italian seasoning, and season generously.
2. Shape into 20 small meatballs.
3. Heat the olive oil in a large skillet over medium heat. Fry the meatballs on both sides until lightly colored, about 4-5 minutes, then lift out of the pan.
4. Add the onions with a pinch of salt, and fry for about 8-10 minutes, until softened and starting to color at the edges.
5. Return the meatballs to the pan and tip in the marinara sauce. Bring to a boil, then turn down to a simmer. Cook for about 10 minutes, until the sauce has thickened, and the meatballs have cooked through.
6. Season to taste, and enjoy!
7. TIP: Vary up the flavor by trying out different spices in the meatballs! Go Thai with some chili paste, Italian with some garlic and lemon zest, or Chinese with soy sauce and ginger!

Nutritional Values, estimated per serving: Macros: Protein 23% / Fat 60% / Carbs 17%; Calories: 463 | Total carbs: 20 g | Net carbs: 16 g | Sugar: 9 g | Protein: 25 g | Fat: 31 g | Saturated fat: 10 g | Cholesterol: 130 mg | Sodium: 463 mg; Glycemic Load: 14.43

LAMB WiTH BLACK OLiVES

gluten-free, lactose-free

 SERVES: 4

 PREP TIME: 10 MINUTES

 COOK TIME: 1 HOUR 30 MINUTES

5 INGREDIENTS

- 1 ½ lb (675 g) stewing lamb, cut into chunks (e.g. leg or shoulder)
- ½ cup (50 g) black olives, pitted
- 1 cup (150 g) cherry tomatoes
- 1 bulb of garlic, separated into cloves and peeled
- 2 sprigs of rosemary

From the pantry
- 2 tbsp olive oil
- 1 tbsp ras el hanout
- Salt and pepper

METHOD:

1. Preheat the oven to 300°F.
2. In a large casserole dish with a lid, mix all the ingredients together and season.
3. Cover with the lid, and bake for about 1 ½ hours, until the lamb is meltingly tender.
4. Serve hot, with the juices from the casserole dish. Enjoy!
5. TIP: You can also try putting some other vegetables into the pot as well! Eggplant, or bell peppers would be very good here.

Nutritional Values, estimated per serving: Macros: Protein 45% / Fat 47% / Carbs 8%; Calories: 335 | Total carbs: 7 g | Net carbs: 5 g | Sugar: 1 g | Protein: 36 g | Fat: 18 g | Saturated fat: 4 g | Cholesterol: 111 mg | Sodium: 531 mg; Glycemic Load: 3.54

TURKEY LETTUCE WRAPS

gluten-free, lactose-free

 SERVES: 2

 PREP TIME: 5 MINUTES

 COOK TIME: 10 MINUTES

5 INGREDIENTS

- ½ lb (225 g) ground turkey
- 1 tbsp Chinese five-spice
- 4 garlic cloves, peeled and chopped
- 2 scallions, sliced, whites and greens separated
- 8 leaves of baby romaine lettuce

From the pantry
- 1 tbsp vegetable oil
- 1 tbsp soy sauce
- 1 tsp harissa chili paste
- Salt and pepper

METHOD:

1. Mix the turkey with the Chinese five-spice, garlic, scallion whites, and chili paste, and season.
2. Heat the vegetable oil in a skillet over medium-high heat, and add the turkey mix. Fry briskly, stirring to break up any lumps, for about 6-8 minutes, until the turkey is cooked. Pour in the soy sauce, and check the seasoning.
3. Put spoonfuls of the spiced turkey into the lettuce leaves, and scatter over the scallion greens. Enjoy!
4. TIP: Serve with a dipping sauce of your choice: hoi sin, scallion sauce, and aioli are all good choices.

Nutritional Values, estimated per serving: Macros: Protein 37% / Fat 55% / Carbs 8%; Calories: 256 | Total carbs: 5 g | Net carbs: 3 g | Sugar: 1 g | Protein: 24 g | Fat: 16 g | Saturated fat: 3 g | Cholesterol: 78 mg | Sodium: 658 mg; Glycemic Load: 3.12

BEEF KOFTA KEBABS

gluten-free, lactose-free

 SERVES: 4

 PREP TIME: 10 MINUTES

 COOK TIME: 10 MINUTES

5 INGREDIENTS

- 1 lb (450 g) ground beef
- 2 onions, peeled, 1 sliced, 1 minced
- 2 cloves of garlic, peeled and minced
- 1 red bell pepper, sliced
- 1 small bunch of parsley, roughly chopped

From the pantry
- 1 tbsp ras el hanout
- 2 tbsp olive oil
- Salt and pepper

METHOD:

1. Mix the ground beef with the minced onion, garlic, ras el hanout, and season.
2. Divide into 8, and shape each piece around a kebab stick, squeezing well so the mixture holds together.
3. Brush the olive oil over the kebabs, and the sliced onion and bell pepper.
4. Get a grill or ridged griddle pan hot, and grill the kebabs together with the vegetables, turning once or twice, until browned and cooked through, and the vegetables are charred in places. About 8-10 minutes.
5. Serve 2 kofta kebabs per person with some of the grilled vegetables alongside. Scatter with parsley and enjoy!
6. TIP: You can try making these with ground lamb as well, or even a mix of lamb and beef!

Nutritional Values, estimated per serving: Macros: Protein 27% / Fat 63% / Carbs 10%; Calories: 347 | Total carbs: 9 g | Net carbs: 6 g | Sugar: 4 g | Protein: 23 g | Fat: 24 g | Saturated fat: 8 g | Cholesterol: 77 mg | Sodium: 379 mg; Glycemic Load: 4.87

VEAL WITH MUSHROOMS

gluten-free, lactose-free

 SERVES: 2

 PREP TIME: 10 MINUTES

 COOK TIME: 10 MINUTES

5 INGREDIENTS

- 2 thin cut veal escalopes, or 4-6 thin slices from the loin, about 8 oz in total
- 6 oz (170 g) mushrooms, sliced
- 2 sprigs of tarragon, stems and leaves separated, finely chopped
- 4 cloves of garlic, peeled and sliced
- ½ cup (120 ml) beef reduction or consomme

From the pantry
- 2 tbsp olive oil
- Salt and pepper

METHOD:

1. Heat the olive oil in a large skillet over medium heat. Add the mushrooms with a pinch of salt and fry until lightly colored, about 5 minutes.
2. Add the garlic and tarragon stems and fry for another 2 minutes.
3. Push the mushrooms to one side of the pan, and add the veal. Turn up the heat, and fry for about 2 minutes each side, until just cooked through.
4. Add the beef reduction, bring to a boil, then immediately take off the heat.
5. Season to taste, and serve immediately, with the mushrooms and veal in the rich gravy.
6. TIP: For a richer, more luxuriant version, try frying in butter instead of olive oil!

Nutritional Values, estimated per serving: Macros: Protein 40% / Fat 53% / Carbs 7%; Calories: 285 | Total carbs: 5 g | Net carbs: 4 g | Sugar: 2 g | Protein: 29 g | Fat: 17 g | Saturated fat: 3 g | Cholesterol: 62 mg | Sodium: 839 mg; Glycemic Load: 6.08

BEEF GOULASH

gluten-free, lactose-free

 SERVES: 4

 PREP TIME: 10 MINUTES

 COOK TIME: 1 HOUR 30 MINUTES

5 INGREDIENTS

- 2 lb (900 g) stewing beef, cut into chunks
- 2 onions, peeled and sliced
- 2 carrots, sliced
- 2 tbsp sweet paprika
- 4 cups (900 ml) of beef broth
- Optional: a few sprigs of fresh thyme

From the pantry
- 1 tbsp tomato paste
- 2 tbsp olive oil
- Salt and pepper

METHOD:

1. Heat half the olive oil in a large pan over medium-high heat and add the beef. Sear on all sides until golden brown, then lift out with a slotted spoon and set aside.
2. Put the rest of the oil in the same pan, then add the onions with a pinch of salt. Fry for about 8-10 minutes, until starting to soften and color at the edges.
3. Return the meat to the pan and add the carrots, paprika and tomato paste. Continue frying for another few minutes, then add the broth.
4. Bring to a boil, then turn down to a simmer and cook until the beef is very tender, about an hour or a little longer.
5. Season to taste, add a little thyme as a garnish if you like, and enjoy!
6. TIP: Try adding some green bell peppers along with the carrots for an interesting variation.

Nutritional Values, estimated per serving: Macros: Protein 53% / Fat 35% / Carbs 12%; Calories: 419 | Total carbs: 14 g | Net carbs: 11 g | Sugar: 6 g | Protein: 56 g | Fat: 17 g | Saturated fat: 5 g | Cholesterol: 150 mg | Sodium: 832 mg; Glycemic Load: 6.27

PAN ROASTED LEMON CHICKEN

gluten-free, lactose-free

 SERVES: 4

 PREP TIME: 10 MINUTES

 COOK TIME: 20 MINUTES

5 INGREDIENTS

- 8 chicken drumsticks, or 4 chicken legs, separated into thighs and drumsticks
- 2 lemons, juice and zest of 1, the other sliced
- ½ cup (50 g) of pitted green olives
- 2 large onions, peeled and sliced
- 3 cups (720 ml) of chicken stock
- Optional: a few sprigs of cilantro or parsley, to garnish

From the pantry
- 1 tbsp olive oil
- 1 tsp Italian seasoning
- Salt and pepper

METHOD:

1. Heat the olive oil in a large skillet over medium-high heat, and add the chicken drumsticks. Fry briskly for about 2-3 minutes each side, until golden brown. Lift out of the pan.
2. Add the onions to the pan with a pinch of salt, and turn the heat down a little. Fry for about 8-10 minutes until softened and starting to color at the edges.
3. Return the chicken to the pan and add the Italian seasoning, olives, lemon zest and juice. Stir to combine, then add the chicken stock.
4. Bring to a boil, then turn down to a simmer. Cook for about 15 minutes, until the chicken is cooked through. Season to taste.
5. Scatter over the herbs, if using, and serve with slices of lemon on the side. Enjoy!
6. TIP: If you can find any preserved lemons, this is a great dish to use them in! Sub out the lemon juice and zest for 1 diced preserved lemon, and reduce the salt.

Nutritional Values, estimated per serving: Macros: Protein 38% / Fat 51% / Carbs 11%; Calories: 587 | Total carbs: 17 g | Net carbs: 15 g | Sugar: 7 g | Protein: 53 g | Fat: 33 g | Saturated fat: 8 g | Cholesterol: 245 mg | Sodium: 1123 mg; Glycemic Load: 5.69

CHAPTER 7
DESSERTS

GREEK YOGURT WITH APPLES

vegetarian, gluten-free

 SERVES: 4

 PREP TIME: 5 MINUTES

 COOK TIME: 5 MINUTES

5 INGREDIENTS

- 2 cups (460 g) of Greek yogurt
- 1 apple, cored and diced
- ½ cup (40 g) walnuts, chopped
- ¼ tsp cinnamon

From the pantry
- 1 tsp olive oil

METHOD:

1. Warm the olive oil in a small skillet over medium-low heat, and add the apples, walnuts and cinnamon.
2. Fry gently for about 5 minutes, until the apple has started to caramelize at the edges. Leave to cool to room temperature.
3. Take 4 small glasses, and split about half the apple mix between them. Put half a cup of Greek yogurt on top, and finish off with the rest of the apple-walnut mix. Enjoy!
4. TIP: This works with other fruit and nuts as well! Try peaches with almonds, or mango and coconut!

Nutritional Values, estimated per serving: Macros: Protein 13% / Fat 61% / Carbs 26%; Calories: 207 | Total carbs: 14 g | Net carbs: 12 g | Sugar: 13 g | Protein: 7 g | Fat: 15 g | Saturated fat: 4 g | Cholesterol: 16 mg | Sodium: 57 mg; Glycemic Load: 2.91

BANANA ICE CREAM

vegan, gluten-free, lactose-free

 SERVES: 2

 PREP TIME: 5 MINUTES

 COOK TIME: 0 MINUTES

 FREEZE TIME: 2 HOURS

5 INGREDIENTS

- 2 medium bananas, peeled
- 2 tbsp almond milk
- ½ cup (40 g) walnuts, chopped and toasted
- ¼ tsp cinnamon

From the pantry
- 1 tsp vanilla extract

METHOD:

1. Freeze the bananas until solid.
2. Put the frozen bananas, cinnamon, vanilla extract, and almond milk into a food processor. Pulse until broken down into slushy ice cream.
3. Return to the freezer for half an hour to firm up again.
4. Top with the walnuts and enjoy!

Nutritional Values, estimated per serving: Macros: Protein 7% / Fat 55% / Carbs 38%; Calories: 309 | Total carbs: 32 g | Net carbs: 27 g | Sugar: 16 g | Protein: 6 g | Fat: 20 g | Saturated fat: 2 g | Cholesterol: 0 mg | Sodium: 10 mg; Glycemic Load: 16.06

BAKED PEACHES WITH YOGURT

vegetarian, gluten-free

 SERVES: 4

 PREP TIME: 5 MINUTES

 COOK TIME: 20 MINUTES

5 INGREDIENTS

- 2 peaches, halved, stone removed
- ¼ cup (20 g) flaked almonds
- 1 tbsp rolled oats
- 4 tbsp Greek yogurt
- 4 sprigs of mint

From the pantry
- 1 tbsp olive oil

METHOD:

1. Preheat the oven to 375°F.
2. Mix the almonds and oats together with the olive oil.
3. Put the peaches into a baking dish, cut side up, and scatter over the almond mixture.
4. Bake for about 20 minutes, until softened and colored.
5. Put a spoon of Greek yogurt on top of each peach half, and scatter over the almond mix remaining in the baking dish. Garnish with mint, and enjoy!
6. TIP: A low-sugar plain frozen yogurt is a good alternative to the Greek yogurt!

Nutritional Values, estimated per serving: Macros: Protein 9% / Fat 56% / Carbs 35%; Calories: 117 | Total carbs: 11 g | Net carbs: 9 g | Sugar: 7 g | Protein: 3 g | Fat: 8 g | Saturated fat: 1 g | Cholesterol: 2 mg | Sodium: 7 mg; Glycemic Load: 4.58

DARK CHOCOLATE ORANGE MOUSSE

vegetarian, gluten-free, lactose-free

 SERVES: 4

 PREP TIME: 10 MINUTES

 COOK TIME: 5 MINUTES

 CHILL TIME: 2 HOURS

5 INGREDIENTS

- 4 eggs, separated
- ½ lb (225 g) dark chocolate, low-sugar or sugar-free
- 1 orange, zest only
- Optional: 1 tbsp diabetes friendly powdered sweetener (e.g. erythritol, monk fruit, stevia)

From the pantry
- A pinch of salt

METHOD:

1. Melt the chocolate in a bain marie or in the microwave. Add a pinch of salt, half the orange zest, the egg yolks, and the sweetener if using, and stir to combine.
2. Whisk the egg whites with an electric whisk until they hold soft peaks.
3. Add about ⅓ of the egg whites to the chocolate, and stir in to loosen the mixture. Fold in the rest of the egg gently, being careful not to knock too much air out.
4. Spoon into 4 glasses, and chill until set. Garnish with the rest of the orange zest, and enjoy!
5. TIP: You can try adding other flavors to the chocolate instead of orange. A little peanut butter, or some cinnamon, or raspberries are all very tasty combinations!

Nutritional Values, estimated per serving: Macros: Protein 10% / Fat 63% / Carbs 27%; Calories: 402 | Total carbs: 28 g | Net carbs: 22 g | Sugar: 14 g | Protein: 10 g | Fat: 28 g | Saturated fat: 15 g | Cholesterol: 165 mg | Sodium: 74 mg; Glycemic Load: 4.03

ORANGE DRIZZLE CAKE

vegetarian, gluten-free

 SERVES: 10

 PREP TIME: 20 MINUTES

 COOK TIME: 40 MINUTES

5 INGREDIENTS

- 2 ½ cups (300 g) almond flour
- 2 small oranges, zest and juice
- 5 eggs
- ½ cup (120 g) butter
- ½ cup (60 g) diabetes friendly powdered sweetener (e.g. erythritol, monk fruit, stevia), plus ¼ cup

From the pantry
- A pinch of salt
- 1 tbsp baking powder
- 1 tsp vanilla extract

METHOD:

1. Preheat the oven to 350°F. Line a 9 x 5-inch loaf tin with parchment paper.
2. Beat the sweetener together with butter until light and creamy.
3. Add the zest and juice of 1 orange, the vanilla extract, and the eggs, and keep beating until well-combined.
4. Add the baking powder, salt, and almond flour, and fold in.
5. Spoon the mix into the loaf tin, smooth the top, and bake for about 40 minutes, until an inserted toothpick comes out clean.
6. Mix the ¼ cup of sweetener with the juice of the other orange.
7. Use the toothpick to poke holes all over the cake, then pour over the orange juice mix.
8. Leave to cool in the tin, then turn out and garnish with the rest of the orange zest. Enjoy!
9. TIP: The same method works for other citrus fruits as well. Try a lemon, lime, or grapefruit drizzle cake!

Nutritional Values, estimated per serving: Macros: Protein 9% / Fat 60% / Carbs 31%; Calories: 248 | Total carbs: 25 g | Net carbs: 22 g | Sugar: 3 g | Protein: 8 g | Fat: 21 g | Saturated fat: 7 g | Cholesterol: 100 mg | Sodium: 54 mg; Glycemic Load: 3.72

TIRAMISU CAKE

vegetarian, gluten-free

 SERVES: 12

 PREP TIME: 15 MINUTES

 CHILL TIME: 4 HOURS

5 INGREDIENTS

- 2 cups (480 ml) heavy cream
- 12 tbsp almond flour
- 4 egg whites
- 6 oz (170 g) dark chocolate, low-sugar or sugar-free, grated
- ½ cup (120 ml) coffee, cooled

From the pantry
- A pinch of salt
- 2 tsp baking powder
- 4 tsp vegetable oil

METHOD:

1. Put 1 tsp of oil into each of 4 ramekins, and swirl to coat.
2. Mix the almond flour with the egg whites, a pinch of salt, and the baking powder, and divide between the ramekins. Microwave on full power for about 90 seconds, until puffed up into little cakes. Turn out from the ramekins and leave to cool.
3. Whip the cream until very thick.
4. Line a 9-inch cake tin with parchment paper.
5. Cut the almond cakes into fingers, and use ⅓ of them to make a thin layer at the bottom.
6. Sprinkle with coffee, top with a layer of whipped cream, and a thin layer of grated chocolate. Repeat twice more, finishing with grated chocolate.
7. Cover, put into the fridge and leave to cool and set. Cut into thick slices and enjoy!
8. TIP: This makes a very adult, darkly bitter tiramisu. If you like it sweeter, add some diabetes-friendly sweetener to the whipped cream.

Nutritional Values, estimated per serving: Macros: Protein 8% / Fat 78% / Carbs 15%; Calories: 277 | Total carbs: 10 g | Net carbs: 7 g | Sugar: 5 g | Protein: 5 g | Fat: 25 g | Saturated fat: 11 g | Cholesterol: 42 mg | Sodium: 35 mg; Glycemic Load: 2.90

CHOCOLATE BLISS BALLS

vegan, gluten-free, lactose-free

 MAKES: 12

 PREP TIME: 10 MINUTES

 COOK TIME: 5 MINUTES

5 INGREDIENTS

- 4 oz (110 g) dark chocolate, low-sugar or sugar-free
- ¾ cup (90 g) of almond flour
- ½ cup (50 g) desiccated coconut, plus extra for rolling
- 2 tbsp cocoa powder, plus extra for rolling
- ½ cup (50 g) finely chopped almonds, plus extra for rolling

From the pantry
- A pinch of salt
- 2 tbsp extra virgin olive oil

METHOD:

1. Melt the chocolate with the olive oil.
2. Mix with the salt, almond flour, chopped almonds, coconut and cocoa powder.
3. Roll into 12 balls, about a tablespoon each, or a little less.
4. Roll 3 in the extra coconut, 3 in the extra cocoa powder, 3 in the extra chopped almonds, and leave 3 plain.
5. Store in the fridge until ready to eat. Enjoy!
6. TIP: These are a great low-carb alternative to chocolate truffles! Serve at the end of a dinner party and amaze your guests!

Nutritional Values, estimated per serving: Macros: Protein 7% / Fat 71% / Carbs 22%; Calories: 176 | Total carbs: 10 g | Net carbs: 7 g | Sugar: 3 g | Protein: 3 g | Fat: 15 g | Saturated fat: 6 g | Cholesterol: 0 mg | Sodium: 30 mg; Glycemic Load: 2.61

MUESLI BARS

vegetarian, lactose-free

 MAKES: 12

 PREP TIME: 10 MINUTES

 COOK TIME: 15 MINUTES

5 INGREDIENTS

- 1 cup (100 g) finely chopped almonds
- ¼ cup (25 g) rolled oats
- ½ cup (50 g) desiccated coconut (unsweetened)
- 3 tbsp almond butter
- 1 egg

From the pantry
- 1 tbsp olive oil
- A pinch of salt

METHOD:

1. Preheat the oven to 350°F. Line an 8 x 8-inch baking dish with parchment.
2. Mix the chopped almonds, oats, and coconut together with a pinch of salt.
3. Whisk the almond butter, oil and egg together, then combine with the almond mix.
4. Press firmly into the prepared baking dish, then bake for about 15 minutes, until golden brown at the edges.
5. Leave to cool in the dish, then turn out and cut into 12 bars. Enjoy!
6. TIP: Mix in whatever dried fruit, seeds, nuts, or low-sugar chocolate chips you want!

Nutritional Values, estimated per serving: Macros: Protein 12% / Fat 68% / Carbs 20%; Calories: 112 | Total carbs: 5 g | Net carbs: 3 g | Sugar: 1 g | Protein: 4 g | Fat: 9 g | Saturated fat: 1 g | Cholesterol: 16 mg | Sodium: 55 mg; Glycemic Load: 3.78

CHEESECAKE

vegetarian, gluten-free

 SERVES: 10

 PREP TIME: 10 MINUTES

 COOK TIME: 1 HOUR MINUTES

5 INGREDIENTS

- 1 ¼ cups (140 g) almond flour
- 5 tbsp butter
- 1 ¼ lb (560 g) cream cheese
- 2 eggs
- ½ cup (60 g) diabetes friendly powdered sweetener (e.g. erythritol, monk fruit, stevia), plus 1 tbsp for the base

From the pantry

- 1 tbsp vanilla extract

METHOD:

1. Preheat the oven to 350°F and line an 8-inch springform cake pan with parchment.
2. Melt the butter and mix together with the almond flour and 1 tbsp of sweetener.
3. Press the crumbly mix into the cake pan, and bake for about 10 minutes, until just starting to color. Remove from the oven and allow to cool a little.
4. Meanwhile, beat the cream cheese with the rest of the sweetener, until light and fluffy.
5. Beat in the eggs and vanilla extract as well, until well mixed.
6. Pour the mixture on top of the cooled base, and smooth the top. Bake for about 40 minutes, until almost completely set, with just a slight wobble.
7. Allow to cool in the pan to room temperature, then refrigerate overnight until set.
8. Turn out carefully from the cake pan, slice and enjoy!
9. TIP: Serve with whatever berries take your fancy! Raspberries, blueberries, and blackberries are especially good!

Nutritional Values, estimated per serving: Macros: Protein 9% / Fat 76% / Carbs 15%; Calories: 301 | Total carbs: 12 g | Net carbs: 10 g | Sugar: 3 g | Protein: 8 g | Fat: 29 g | Saturated fat: 15 g | Cholesterol: 103 mg | Sodium: 262 mg; Glycemic Load: 1.59

PEANUT BUTTER COOKIES

vegetarian, lactose-free

 MAKES: 12

 PREP TIME: 5 MINUTES

 COOK TIME: 15 MINUTES

5 INGREDIENTS

- 1 cup (250 g) of peanut butter
- 1 egg
- 1 tbsp oats
- 1 tbsp low-sugar chocolate chips
- ¼ cup (30 g) diabetes-friendly powdered sweetener (e.g. erythritol, monk fruit, stevia)

From the pantry

- 1 tsp vanilla extract
- A pinch of salt

METHOD:

1. Preheat the oven to 350°F. Line a baking sheet with a piece of parchment paper.
2. Mix all the ingredients together, then divide into 12 portions.
3. Roll each portion into a rough ball, and place onto the baking sheet. Press down to flatten each one.
4. Bake for about 12-15 minutes, until starting to turn golden at the edges.
5. Cool on a wire rack, then enjoy!
6. TIP: For regular chocolate chip cookies, just use dairy butter instead of the PB!

Nutritional Values, estimated per serving: Macros: Protein 14% / Fat 64% / Carbs 22%; Calories: 144 | Total carbs: 9 g | Net carbs: 8 g | Sugar: 2 g | Protein: 6 g | Fat: 12 g | Saturated fat: 3 g | Cholesterol: 16 mg | Sodium: 96 mg; Glycemic Load: 1.26

FROZEN YOGURT POPSICLES WITH RASPBERRIES

vegetarian, gluten-free,

 MAKES: 8

PREP TIME: 10 MINUTES

COOK TIME: 5 MINUTES

FREEZE TIME: 4 HOURS

5 INGREDIENTS

- 2 cups (460 g) of Greek yogurt
- 1 cup (~230 ml) heavy cream
- 1 egg white
- ¼ cup (30 g) diabetes-friendly powdered sweetener (e.g. erythritol, monk fruit, stevia), plus 1 tbsp
- 1 cup (125 g) raspberries

METHOD:

1. Put the raspberries into a pan with 1 tbsp of sweetener and a small splash of water. Set over a low heat and cook for about 5 minutes, just until the raspberries have collapsed into a rough sauce. Leave to cool, then split between the bases of 8 popsicle molds.
2. Beat the egg white with the sweetener until soft peaks have formed.
3. Whip the cream until stiff.
4. Fold both gently into the yogurt, and divide between the popsicle molds, topping the raspberries.
5. Freeze until set, at least 4 hours.
6. Unmold the popsicles, and enjoy!
7. TIP: You can also try the same method with different berries. Blackberries and strawberries are also good in this recipe.

Nutritional Values, estimated per serving: Macros: Protein 9% / Fat 61% / Carbs 30%; Calories: 125 | Total carbs: 12 g | Net carbs: 11 g | Sugar: 4 g | Protein: 3 g | Fat: 10 g | Saturated fat: 6 g | Cholesterol: 39 mg | Sodium: 44 mg; Glycemic Load: 1.76

HOMEMADE BLACKBERRY ICE CREAM

Vegetarian, gluten-free

 SERVES: 4

PREP TIME: 10 MINUTES

 COOK TIME: 5 MINUTES

 CHILL TIME: 2 HOURS

5 INGREDIENTS

- 2 cups (250 g) blackberries
- 1 lemon, juice only
- ¾ cup (180 ml) heavy cream
- 1 tbsp vodka
- ¼ cup (30 g) diabetes-friendly powdered sweetener (e.g. erythritol, monk fruit, stevia)

METHOD:

1. Put all the ingredients into a blender, along with ¾ cup of water.
2. Blend until very smooth, and strain to remove the seeds.
3. Chill the mixture, then process in an ice cream machine.
4. Serve immediately for soft-serve consistency, or freeze for an extra hour for a firmer texture. Enjoy!
5. TIP: For a lighter version, try replacing the cream with ¾ cup more water, for a blackberry sorbet.

Nutritional Values, estimated per serving: Macros: Protein 3 % / Fat 62% / Carbs 35%; Calories: 171 | Total carbs: 19 g | Net carbs: 15 g | Sugar: 5 g | Protein: 2 g | Fat: 14 g | Saturated fat: 9 g | Cholesterol: 51 mg | Sodium: 15 mg; Glycemic Load: 3.34

POMEGRANATE JELLO

gluten-free, lactose-free

 SERVES: 4

 PREP TIME: 5 MINUTES

 COOK TIME: 5 MINUTES

 CHILL TIME: 2 HOURS

5 INGREDIENTS

- 1 large pomegranates, juice from ¾, the other quarter broken into arils
- 1 packet powdered gelatin (¼ oz, ~7 g)
- 1 tbsp diabetes-friendly powdered sweetener (e.g. erythritol, monk fruit, stevia)
- ¼ cup (30 ml) heavy cream
- Optional: 2 tbsp unsalted pistachios, roughly crushed

METHOD:

1. Put the pomegranate juice, sweetener, and 1 cup water into a saucepan.
2. Heat over medium heat, stirring until the gelatin has dissolved, about 3-4 minutes.
3. Divide the mixture between 4 glasses, and chill for at least 2 hours, until set.
4. Whip the cream, and put a teaspoon on each jello glass. Scatter over the reserved arils, and the pistachios, if using, and enjoy!
5. TIP: You can use the same method to make jello with other fruit juices as well. Just be sure to dilute with water to make sure it's not too sugary!

Nutritional Values, estimated per serving: Macros: Protein 12% / Fat 21% / Carbs 67%; Calories: 116 | Total carbs: 22 g | Net carbs: 17 g | Sugar: 15 g | Protein: 4 g | Fat: 3 g | Saturated fat: <1 g | Cholesterol: 0 mg | Sodium: 7 mg; Glycemic Load: 8.58

SPICED STRAWBERRIES

vegan, gluten-free, lactose-free

 SERVES: 2

 PREP TIME: 5 MINUTES

 COOK TIME: 0 MINUTES

5 INGREDIENTS

- 2 cups (300 g) strawberries, hulled and chopped
- 1 small bunch of basil, roughly chopped

From the pantry
- Freshly ground black pepper

METHOD:

1. Divide the strawberries between 2 bowls, and scatter over the basil.
2. Grind some fresh black pepper over, and enjoy!
3. TIP: For extra richness, serve with a little whipped cream on the side!

Nutritional Values, estimated per serving: Macros: Protein 7% / Fat 8% / Carbs 85%; Calories: 49 | Total carbs: 12 g | Net carbs: 9 g | Sugar: 7 g | Protein: 1 g | Fat: <1 g | Saturated fat: <1 g | Cholesterol: 0 mg | Sodium: 2 mg; Glycemic Load: 4.08

BANANA CUSTARD PUDDING

vegetarian, gluten-free

 SERVES: 4

 PREP TIME: 5 MINUTES

 COOK TIME: 10 MINUTES

 CHILL TIME: 2 HOURS

5 INGREDIENTS

- 1 small banana, mashed
- ¾ cup (180 ml) heavy cream, plus ¼ cup extra to whip
- 4 egg yolks
- ½ cup (120 ml) almond milk
- 2 tbsp diabetes-friendly powdered sweetener (e.g. erythritol, monk fruit, stevia)
- Optional: 1 tsp chopped nuts and/or mint sprigs, to serve

From the pantry
- 1 tsp vanilla extract

METHOD:

1. Put the cream, almond milk, sweetener, and vanilla extract into a pan and heat until just simmering. Turn off the heat.
2. Meanwhile, mix the banana with the egg yolks.
3. Pour half the hot cream onto the egg yolk mixture, whisking continuously. Then pour the egg yolk mix back into the saucepan.
4. Set over a very low heat, and cook for about 5 minutes, whisking continuously, until the mixture thickens.
5. Divide the mix between 4 glasses, and chill for at least 2 hours, until completely set.
6. Whip the remaining cream, and use it to top the banana pudding.
7. Optionally garnish with chopped nuts and mint, and enjoy!
8. TIP: Adding some warming spices to the cream is a nice winter twist on this recipe. Try nutmeg, cinnamon, or ginger!

Nutritional Values, estimated per serving: Macros: Protein 7% / Fat 72% / Carbs 21%; Calories: 250 | Total carbs: 14 g | Net carbs: 13 g | Sugar: 6 g | Protein: 4 g | Fat: 22 g | Saturated fat: 12 g | Cholesterol: 246 mg | Sodium: 42 mg; Glycemic Load: 5.59

MEAL PLANS

WEEK 1

Meal plan

	BREAKFAST	LUNCH	DINNER	SNACK OR DESSERT
Monday	Almond Pancakes with Strawberries	Spanish Gazpacho	Japanese Chicken-Ginger Meatballs	Greek Yogurt with Apples
Tuesday	Smoked Salmon Breakfast Salad	Spicy Chicken Salad	Chickpea Curry	Banana Ice Cream
Wednesday	Mexican Scrambled Eggs	Chilled Cucumber Yogurt Soup	Grilled Mackerel	Chocolate Bliss Balls
Thursday	Super Green Smoothie	Asian Beef Salad	Red Lentil Dhal	Muesli Bars
Friday	Summer Frittata	Roasted Cherry Tomato Soup	Turkey Patties with Salad	Frozen Yogurt Popsicles
Saturday	Shakshuka	Italian White Bean Salad	Keralan Fish Curry	Dark Chocolate Orange Mousse
Sunday	Spinach and Feta Omelet	Asparagus Spinach Soup	Moroccan Beef Tagine	Baked Peaches with Yogurt

Grocery list

Fruit and vegetables

- Red onions x 5 recipes
- Onions x 5 recipes
- Scallions x 2 recipes
- Shallots
- Leeks
- Green bell peppers x 2 recipes
- Red bell peppers
- Tomatoes x 3 recipes
- Cherry tomatoes x 4 recipes
- Zucchini x 2 recipes
- Asparagus
- Carrots
- Pumpkin
- Arugula x 3 recipes
- Spinach x 4 recipes
- Cucumber x 4 recipes
- Ginger x 4 recipes
- Garlic x 4 recipes

- Red chilis x 2 recipes
- Strawberries
- Raspberries
- Bananas
- Apples
- Peaches
- Lemons x 3 recipes
- Limes
- Orange

Herbs and spices

- Tarragon
- Mint
- Parsley x 3 recipes
- Cilantro x 4 recipes
- Basil x 2 recipes
- Dill x 2 recipes
- Cinnamon x 2 recipes

Pantry staples and dry packaged goods

- Almond flour x 2 recipes
- Desiccated coconut x 2 recipes
- Cocoa powder
- Chopped almonds x 5 recipes
- Oats x 2 recipes
- Whole grain bread
- Cashew nuts x 2 recipes
- Walnuts x 2 recipes
- Sesame seeds
- Dried apricots
- Red lentils
- Dark chocolate x 2 recipes
- Artificial sweetener x 2 recipes

Standard pantry

- Olive oil
- Extra virgin olive oil
- Vegetable oil
- Vinegar

- Soy sauce
- Baking powder
- Chili paste
- Ras el hanout
- Garam masala
- Italian seasoning
- Salt
- Pepper

Cans, jars, bottles, preserves

- Vanilla extract x 2 recipes
- Thai red curry paste
- Teriyaki sauce
- Dill pickles
- Green olives
- Capers
- Peanut butter
- Almond butter
- Tomato paste
- Canned tomatoes x 3 recipes
- Canned white beans
- Canned chickpeas
- Chicken stock x 2 recipes

Meat and fish

- Chicken breasts
- Lean beef steak x 2 recipes
- Ground chicken
- Ground turkey
- White fish fillets
- Mackerel fillets
- Smoked Salmon

Dairy and eggs

- Eggs x 10 recipes
- Greek yogurt x 5 recipes
- Feta cheese x 3 recipes
- Almond milk
- Heavy Cream

WEEK 2

Meal plan

	BREAKFAST	LUNCH	DINNER	SNACK OR DESSERT
Monday	Avocado Toast with Asparagus	Zucchini Basil Soup	Lamb with Black Olives	Muesli Bars
Tuesday	Overnight Oats	Fennel, Orange, Arugula Salad	Steamed Mussels	Beetroot Dip with Crudités
Wednesday	Breakfast Salad with Salmon	Chilled Cucumber Yogurt Soup	Lentils with Grilled Chicken	Strawberries with Black Pepper
Thursday	Summer Frittata	Green Beans with Almonds	Fish Skewers	Tzatziki with crudités
Friday	Cocoa Peanut Chia Pudding	Summer Avocado Chicken Salad	Vietnamese Summer Rolls	Peanut Butter Cookies
Saturday	Broccoli Muffins with Cheddar	Roasted Cherry Tomato Soup	Shrimp Salad with Avocado	Blackberry Ice Cream
Sunday	Noodle Breakfast Broth	Apple and Celery Salad	Mexican Chili Bean Soup	Banana Custard Pudding

Grocery list

Fruit and vegetables

- Onions x 2 recipes
- Scallions
- French beans
- Red cabbage
- Green bell peppers
- Yellow bell peppers
- Avocado x 4 recipes
- Fennel
- Tomatoes
- Cherry tomatoes x 2 recipes
- Zucchini x 2 recipes
- Broccoli
- Bok choy
- Asparagus
- Peas
- Carrots x 4 recipes
- Celery x 3 recipes

- Beetroot
- Arugula x 3 recipes
- Romaine lettuce
- Cucumber x 4 recipes
- Garlic x 8 recipes
- Strawberries
- Raspberries
- Bananas
- Apples
- Lemons x 8 recipes
- Limes
- Oranges
- Blackberries

Herbs and spices

- Mint x 2 recipes
- Rosemary
- Parsley x 5 recipes
- Cilantro
- Basil x 4 recipes

- Dill
- Garlic powder

Pantry staples and dry packaged goods

- Desiccated coconut
- Chia seeds
- Cocoa powder
- Chopped almonds x 3 recipes
- Oats x 3 recipes
- Whole grain bread
- Konjac noodles
- Walnuts x 2 recipes
- Brown lentils
- Dark chocolate
- Artificial sweetener x 3 recipes
- Rice paper

Standard pantry

- Olive oil
- Extra virgin olive oil
- Vegetable oil
- Vinegar
- Baking powder
- Vanilla extract
- Chili paste
- Soy sauce
- Ras el hanout
- Garam masala
- Italian seasoning
- Salt
- Pepper

Cans, jars, bottles, preserves

- Vodka
- Mayonnaise
- Black olives x 2 recipes
- Peanut butter x 2 recipes
- Almond butter
- Tahini
- Canned chili tomatoes Canned kidney beans
- Chicken stock x 2 recipes
- Vegetable stock

Meat and fish

- Chicken tenders
- Chicken breasts
- Lean lamb steak
- Ground beef
- White fish fillets
- Smoked salmon
- Live mussels
- Shrimp

Dairy and eggs

- Eggs x 8 recipes
- Greek yogurt x 6 recipes
- Feta cheese
- Cheddar cheese
- Almond milk x 2 recipes
- Milk
- Heavy cream x 2 recipes

WEEK 3

Meal plan

	BREAKFAST	LUNCH	DINNER	SNACK OR DESSERT
Monday	Super Green Smoothie	Asparagus Spinach Soup	Beef Kofta Kebabs	Peanut Butter Cookies
Tuesday	Spanish Tortilla	Asian Beef Salad	Cauliflower Piccata	Orange Drizzle Cake
Wednesday	Baked Avocado with Eggs	Broccoli and Stilton Soup	Tilapia with Cauliflower Rice	Baked Peaches with Yogurt
Thursday	Gribiche on Toast	Apple and Celery Salad	Pan Roasted Lemon Chicken	Muesli Bars
Friday	Cauliflower Hash Browns	Spanish Gazpacho	Veal with Mushrooms	Strawberries with Black Pepper
Saturday	Avocado Toast with Rye Bread	Spicy Chicken Salad	Grilled Tofu with Soba Noodles	Greek Yogurt with Apples
Sunday	Eggs Florentine	Cauliflower Soup	Garlic Shrimp Spaghetti	Beetroot Dip with Crudités

Grocery list

Fruit and vegetables

- Red onions x 2 recipes
- Onions x 6 recipes
- Scallions
- Shallots x 2 recipes
- Leeks
- Cauliflower x 4 recipes
- Green bell peppers x 2 recipes
- Red bell peppers x 3 recipes
- Tomatoes
- Cherry tomatoes
- Broccoli x 2 recipe
- Avocado x 2 recipe
- Asparagus
- Beetroot
- Shiitake mushrooms
- Mushrooms
- Celery
- Potatoes x 2 recipe
- Spinach x 5 recipes
- Romaine lettuce
- Cucumber x 2 recipes
- Ginger
- Garlic x 8 recipes
- Red chilis
- Strawberries
- Apples x 2 recipes
- Lemons x 8 recipes
- Limes
- Oranges
- Peaches

Herbs and spices

- Tarragon x 2 recipes
- Parsley x 5 recipes
- Mint
- Basil
- Cinnamon

- Garlic powder
- Red pepper flakes

Pantry staples and dry packaged goods
- Almond flour
- Desiccated coconut Chopped almonds x 2 recipes
- Oats x 3 recipes
- Whole grain bread x 2 recipes
- Whole grain muffins
- Soba noodles
- Konjac noodles
- Cashew nuts x 2 recipes
- Peanuts
- Walnuts x 2 recipes
- Sesame seeds
- Pumpkin seeds
- Dark chocolate x 2 recipes
- Artificial sweetener x 2 recipes

Standard pantry
- Olive oil
- Extra virgin olive oil
- Vegetable oil
- Vinegar
- Baking powder
- Vanilla extract
- Chili paste
- Ras el hanout
- Garam masala
- Whole wheat flour

- Italian seasoning
- Salt
- Pepper

Cans, jars, bottles, preserves
- Mayonnaise
- Dill pickle
- Green olives
- Capers x 2 recipes
- Peanut butter x 2 recipes
- Almond butter
- Tahini x 2 recipe
- Chicken stock x 2 recipes
- Beef broth
- Vegetable stock x 2 recipe

Meat and fish
- Chicken breasts
- Lean beef steak
- Chicken legs
- Ground beef
- Veal escalopes
- Shrimp
- Tilapia fillets
- **Dairy and eggs**
- Eggs x 8 recipes
- Greek yogurt x 4 recipes
- Cream cheese
- Stilton cheese
- Butter x 2 recipe
- Tofu

WEEK 4

Meal plan

	BREAKFAST	LUNCH	DINNER	SNACK OR DESSERT
Monday	Almond Pancakes with Strawberries	Fennel, Orange, Arugula Salad	Fishcakes	Orange Drizzle Cake
Tuesday	Smashed Avocado with Edamame	Summer Avocado Chicken Salad	Buddha Bowl	Tzatziki with crudités
Wednesday	Mexican Scrambled Eggs	Quinoa Tabbouleh	Beef Goulash	Frozen Yogurt Popsicles
Thursday	Super Green Smoothie	Asian Beef Salad	Moroccan Eggplant	Strawberries with Black Pepper
Friday	Summer Frittata	Green Beans with Almonds	Teriyaki Salmon	Blackberry Ice Cream
Saturday	Shakshuka	Fattoush	Meatballs in Tomato Sauce	Banana Custard Pudding
Sunday	Spinach and Feta Omelet	Zucchini Basil Soup	Thai Baked Chicken	Chocolate Bliss Balls

Grocery list

Fruit and vegetables

- Red onions x 3 recipes
- Onions x 3 recipes
- Leeks
- Bok choy
- Green bell peppers 2 x recipes
- Avocado x 3 recipe
- Green beans
- Tomatoes x 4 recipes
- Cherry tomatoes
- Zucchini x 2 recipes
- Eggplant
- Asparagus
- Broccoli
- Pea sprouts
- Peas

- Fennel
- Carrots x 2 recipes
- Celery x 2 recipe
- Pumpkin
- Arugula x 2 recipes
- Spinach x 2 recipes
- Romaine lettuce
- Cucumber x 3 recipes
- Edamame beans
- Ginger
- Garlic x 4 recipes
- Red chilis
- Strawberries x 2 recipes
- Raspberries
- Bananas
- Lemons x 6 recipes
- Limes x 2 recipes
- Oranges x 2 recipes

- Blackberries
- **<u>Herbs and spices</u>**
- Parsley x 4 recipes
- Chives
- Mint x 2 recipe
- Cilantro
- Basil x 2 recipes
- Dill x 2 recipes
- Sweet paprika

Pantry staples and dry packaged goods

- Almond flour x 4 recipes
- Desiccated coconut
- Cocoa powder
- Chopped almonds x 3 recipes
- Quinoa
- Whole grain bread
- Whole grain pita
- Fresh breadcrumbs
- Cashew nuts
- Walnuts
- Sesame seeds
- Dark chocolate
- Artificial sweetener x 4 recipes

Standard pantry

- Olive oil
- Extra virgin olive oil
- Vegetable oil
- Vinegar
- Baking powder
- Vanilla extract
- Chili paste

- Ras el hanout
- Tomato paste
- Garam masala
- Italian seasoning
- Salt
- Pepper

Cans, jars, bottles, preserves

- Vodka
- Thai red curry paste
- Teriyaki sauce
- Black olives
- Peanut butter
- Roasted red peppers Canned tomatoes x 2 recipes
- Canned chickpeas
- Beef stock
- Vegetable stock

Meat and fish

- Chicken breasts
- Lean beef steak x 2 recipes
- Chicken thighs
- Ground pork
- Salmon fillets x 2 recipes

Dairy and eggs

- Eggs x 10 recipes
- Greek yogurt x 4 recipes
- Feta cheese x 3 recipes
- Almond milk
- Heavy cream x 3 recipes
- Butter